REFORMission

MARK DRISCOLL

REFORMission

REACHING OUT WITHOUT
SELLING OUT

ZONDERVAN.com/
AUTHORTRACKER
follow your favorite authors

ZONDERVAN

Reformission
Copyright © 2004 by Mars Hill Church

Previously published as *The Radical Reformission*

Requests for information should be addressed to:

Zondervan, *Grand Rapids, Michigan 49530*

This edition: ISBN 978-0-310-51500-5

All Scripture quotations, unless otherwise indicated, are taken from The Holy
Bible, *New International Version®, NIV®.* Copyright © 1973, 1978, 1984 by Biblica,
Inc.™ Used by permission. All rights reserved worldwide.

Any Internet addresses (websites, blogs, etc.) and telephone numbers in this
book are offered as a resource. They are not intended in any way to be or imply
an endorsement by Zondervan, nor does Zondervan vouch for the content of
these sites and numbers for the life of this book.

Cover design: Micah Kandros Design
Cover photo: Veer
Interior photo: Doug Irvine
Interior design: Matthew Van Zomeren

Printed in the United States of America

13 14 15 16 17 18 19 20 /DCI/ 14 13 12 11 10 9 8 7 6 5 4 3 2 1

To Grace

CONTENTS

PART 2: LOVING YOUR NEIGHBOR IN THE CULTURE

PREFACE

I wrote and published this book nearly a decade ago, at the very beginning of my ministry career, in the early years of Mars Hill Church. Despite our starting with no formal theological training, completely broke, without paid staff for the first three years, and trying to reach the least-churched demographic — young single men — in one of America's least-churched cities, the big ideas in this book have helped shape a gospel culture that has proven fruitful, by God's grace. We started as a home Bible study and grew slowly at first, taking a few years to reach even a few hundred.

We are now one church in fourteen locations, spread across four states, and likely will be more than that by the time this preface is printed. We are ministering in urban and suburban contexts and reaching people of multiple races, incomes, education levels, and life stages. We are now one of the fastest-growing and largest churches in America. Most of our attendees and converts are single, college-educated urbanites, including an army of young men who were part of the fools' parade until Jesus grabbed them by the collar. People are getting married by the hundreds every year, and we've got a few thousand kids so far, with more entering the world every day.

We have gone from nothing to amazing without theological compromise, without a huge influx of cash, and without a cultural change in our cities, where people are still unlikely to go to church and love Jesus. We've never had an evangelism department, evangelism method, or even evangelistic events. Our sermons are still long (really long), and we generally work through books of the Bible, talking a lot about sin, repentance, and the wrath of God. Our buildings are still not epic, our parking is still a joke without a punchline, we've made enough mistakes to sink the church ten times over, and, to be honest, we are still trying to get many of our ministries (such as children and students) anywhere near the level of other churches our size across the nation, most of which resemble small outposts for Disneyland. And we have not grown much from transfer attendance, because most of our people live in highly secular urban areas and got saved and baptized at our church. Heck, we are even Reformed, which is a theological tribe that, frankly, is quite lousy at evangelism. (Reformed folks tend to have a theology of evangelism that often doesn't translate into a reality of evangelism.)

We are not the smartest. We are not the richest. We are not the coolest. So it's no surprise that many people often ask, "What's the secret?"

It's no secret.

The gospel is true. Jesus is alive. The Holy Spirit is at work. It is possible to reach out without selling out.

The key is God's grace and avoiding nonbiblical theological hangups, outdated traditions, and ineffective ministry philosophies that put water on the fire of the gospel. The gospel will inspire God's people to live on God's mission for God's glory, if we don't hinder it. The gospel is the power of God to save, if we release it. The gospel is a light that attracts the lost, if we get rid of the churchianity bushel under which it's hiding. Getting out good news should not be so complicated. The problem is never the gospel; the problem is always us. Either we get the gospel wrong, or we don't get the gospel out.

So we have to repent. Repentance allows us to get out of Jesus' way and allows him to lead and his people to follow on mission together in the culture.

Many years after writing this, my first book, I am happy to report that in God's grace, its big ideas got us going in a direction that now has a lot of momentum. Jesus is alive, and he is faithful.

— Mark Driscoll, November 2012

ACKNOWLEDGMENTS

I want to thank those people who have had the biggest impact on my life and ministry:

Thanks to my mom and pop for giving their lives to make mine great.
Thanks to my bride, Grace, for buying me the Bible I teach from and for pointing me to Jesus.
Thanks to my children for the joy it is to be their dad.
Thanks to my mother-in-law and father-in-law for their support.
Thanks to Greg Kappas for giving a young punk a shot at ministry.
Thanks to Antioch Bible Church for funding our church plant.
Thanks to Lief Moi and Mike Gunn for helping me plant Mars Hill Church.
Thanks to David Nicholas for joining me in founding the Acts 29 Network and for serving Christ with me.
Thanks to the Acts 29 church planters for their courage.
Thanks to the members of Mars Hill Church for allowing me to be their pastor.
Thanks to the elders of Mars Hill for their devotion.
Thanks to Jon and Esther Phelps for their kindness.
Thanks to Brad and Diane Sessler for their selflessness.
Thanks to Bob Buford, Linda Stanley, Dave Travis, and Brad Smith at Leadership Network for their generosity.

Thanks to Lesslie Newbigin for his prophetic voice.

Thanks to the Puritans for their example.

Thanks to Dr. Gerry Breshears for helping shape my theology.

Thanks to Charles Haddon Spurgeon for his inspiration.

Thanks to John, Paul, and the other Beatles at Zondervan for publishing this book.

Thanks to Jesus for the empty tomb and for something to preach.

INTRODUCTION

My Personal Reformission and
the Emerging Reformission Movement

Culturally, I am Irish, which means I have two emotions: angry and asleep. I was raised as the oldest of five kids in a hardworking, blue-collar Catholic family near the airport in Seattle, Washington. It was a Norman Rockwell–Precious Moments kind of neighborhood just up the hill from the strip clubs and the hunting grounds of the Green River Killer and Ted Bundy.

Growing up, I thought that as long as I believed in a nebulous Sky Fairy named God and was a decent, moral person outperforming those below me on the ethical food chain, I would end my life hearing the old theme song from *The Jeffersons* television show and be "movin' on up" to heaven with all the other good guys. So I worked hard through high school and graduated Most Likely to Succeed and student body president. I was very proud to have never drunk alcohol, smoked a cigarette, tried a drug, or voted Republican.

Upon graduation, I was awarded a few scholarships that enabled me to be the first person in my family to go to college. So, wanting to get out of the city and try something new, I moved about three hundred miles away to Washington State University, which is tucked away in the wheatfields of eastern Washington. The university was far away from big city life, complete with cows, instead of prostitutes, standing around like dumb meat.

Without a car and majoring in boredom, I began reading a nice Bible my high school girlfriend had given me as a graduation present. She was a pastor's daughter who, in retrospect, should not have been dating me. Nonetheless, she has turned out to be an amazing wife who is the embodiment of her name, Grace. To this day, I preach each Sunday from the Bible she gave me, even on the Sundays when, as a good professional hypocrite, I tell the unmarried people never to date non-Christians.

After a bad few weeks of a frat experience that landed me in the freshman equivalent of purgatory — a dorm — I sat down to read the Gospels. Frankly, they seemed boring because they kept saying the same thing. I wondered if the Bible wasn't written by an old man with dementia, or by a young man who had gone to my "publick skewl." As I continued to read, Jesus seemed okay, but the guys I really liked — because of their self-control and strength — were the denominational leaders of that day: the Pharisees. They were about the only guys in the cast of characters with any guts. I identified with them and was convinced they were the good guys in the story ... until they killed Jesus. I wasn't much of a theologian at the time, but murdering Jesus did seem like a bad move.

Moving on, as Peter says, I found the writings of Paul hard to understand. His obsession with sin reminded me of a DEA dog at the airport sniffing around for drugs with tail-wagging enthusiasm. My problem was that I thought sin was something you *do,* not understanding that sin is something you *are,* like being French Canadian. To me, sins were terrible things that very bad people do, such as rape, murder, drug dealing, and what my construction-worker dad called being antiunion. Consequently, Paul seemed to be going after bad people. And since I was a good person, I skipped Paul and started reading John's Revelation. It sounded eerily similar to the revelations an altar-boy buddy of mine had reported seeing while assisting our priest with a Mass, shortly after smoking lots of marijuana.

In my first college philosophy class, I read Augustine, who said that sin naturally flows from our polluted hearts like sewage out of a culvert. He explained that the root of sin is pride and that the worst sins include things like false morality and autonomy from God. This was, I believe, God's extending to me the right foot of fellowship.

I then read the entire New Testament over the course of the next few weeks. God opened my eyes to the fact that I was a Pharisee and that the worst sinners are often the most moral and spiritual people who, like I was doing, pursue righteousness apart from Jesus. As I was sitting on my dorm bed, the words of Romans 1:6, "And you also are among those who are called to belong to Jesus Christ," sounded in my head like an alarm. I realized that God had been pursuing me and was, in that moment, screaming into the three pounds of meat between my ears that I belong to Jesus.

That week, I started teaching my first Bible study. At the time, *The Simpsons* on television was all the rage among drunken college guys. My dorm room had cable television, also known as evangelistic bait. So I gathered the guys from my dorm floor together and told them they could watch the show in our room if they also attended my Bible study beforehand. Much to my surprise, about ten guys showed up.

It then dawned on me that I had been a Christian for only a few days, had never been in a Bible study, and did not really know anything in the Bible other than the fact that I sucked and that Jesus is God. So I told the guys they could ask me any question about the Bible and I would take the following week to research the answer, since I didn't have any answers yet. This was my first ministry, and it inspired me to begin buying commentaries, reference materials, theology texts, apologetics books, and the like, which were more interesting by far than most of my classes. For example, I had a class in women's studies in which I learned that men are a plague ruining the world and that I needed to get in touch with my feminine side, which made about as much sense as telling a dog to get in touch with its feline side.

Shortly thereafter, I found a good church that met my criteria. First, the pastor was a man who had been in the military and knew how to kill people in self-defense. Second, he taught through the Bible verse by verse, so that I could learn to trust the Scriptures and to love Jesus without feeling like we had a thinly veiled homosexual relationship. I attended their men's retreat in Idaho with other hairy image-bearers of God, and spent a weekend talking about things such as sex, pipe tobacco, and monotheism. It was about the best weekend I could remember having in my life at that time.

Late one night during the retreat, I went down to the river and was compelled by God to kneel for some time in prayer. Then it happened! He spoke to me and told me what to do with the days between my birth and judgment — in other words, my life. He told me to lead men, preach Scripture, plant churches, marry Grace, and trust him. So I married Grace, began studying Scripture with the enthusiasm of a glutton at a buffet, and started preparing myself to become a pastor who does not go to jail for doing something stupid. To pay the bills, I edited the opinions section of the campus newspaper, writing inflammatory columns that led to debates, radio interviews, and even a few bomb threats — which was wonderful, because the only thing worse than dying is living a boring life.

After graduation, Grace and I moved back to Seattle and began visiting churches. We finally settled into a large suburban church where I felt at home because it met my criteria. First, the pastor (who looked like Mr. T) had been an NFL linebacker and knew how to kill people in self-defense. Second, he taught the Bible verse by verse in a real way, one that enabled me to have a relationship with Jesus that did not feel like he was my lifelong prom date.

Grace and I volunteered in college ministry for a few years and met Lief Moi, who later became a dear friend and a founding elder at our church. He hosted a weekly, three-hour, national Christian call-in radio program that focused on cultural issues and evangelizing lost people. I spent the next six years cohosting the radio show and learning a great deal about the views and struggles of young non-Christians and new Christians. After a few years of serving at the church, we were sent out to plant our own church in urban Seattle, where Grace and I were living and had grown up.

The church — Mars Hill Church — started in my living room with about a dozen people: a few great families and some college-age folks. In the fall of 1996, a week before my twenty-sixth birthday, we launched the church with about 150 people. Shortly thereafter, I received a phone call from a young pastor named Chris Seay, who was involved with an organization called Leadership Network. He asked about our church and informed me of a conference for young pastors that he was helping to lead at the Mount Hermon Conference Center in California. The conference included Dieter Zander, who was on staff at Willow Creek at the time, and Tim Celek, with whom Dieter had written a book, *Inside the Soul of a New Generation.*

I had never met another young senior pastor and had never been to a pastors' conference, but I decided to accept their offer to participate. They gave me a main session in which to rant for about an hour. The conference theme was the oh-so-trendy — and now somewhat embarrassing — topic of Generation X. Approximately five hundred young pastors from across the nation showed up — each one, myself included, with some sort of facial hair, like a peculiar Esau-esque antishaving cult.

My sermon, "The Flight from God," was on the emerging culture of postmodernism. That one message quite unexpectedly launched a national platform. To my surprise and delight, it ended up being the bestselling tape from any event at the conference center that year. Upon my return home, my phone began ringing with calls from media outlets ranging from National Public Radio and *Mother Jones* magazine, to *The 700 Club* television program, *Christianity Today* magazine, and a host of others — all wanting interviews. Then other conferences began sending requests for me to travel and teach across the United States and Canada, and denominations began to request consultations.

A team of young pastors, including myself, was then formed by Leadership Network, and we flew around the country speaking to other pastors about the emerging culture and the emerging church, in conjunction with older theoreticians, such as Leonard Sweet, Stan Grenz, Sally Morgenthaler, George Hunsberger, and Tom Sine. I must confess that I felt like the short guy in *The Wizard of Oz* standing behind the curtain, pulling levers to proliferate the illusion of an empire, since our new church was broke and was running with fewer than two hundred people. When the secretaries for high-powered people called to speak with me, I was answering the phone at home in my underwear, since we didn't even have an office or a secretary.

The travel, combined with my pastoral ignorance and the work of trying to grow a young church, quickly became wearying. Furthermore, the speaking team of young pastors eventually split into various networks. Rather than trying to help build any of the newly emerging networks, I chose to stick close to home and concentrate on my marriage, young children, and needy church. At this time, God spoke to me very clearly, rebuking me for lacking the humility, ministry success, or wisdom to be traveling, writing books, and acting like a rock star flying around the country to stand on stages before crowds.

In retrospect, my trip to the woodshed with the Father probably saved my life. At the time, there was a growing national buzz about the emerging church in the emerging culture. This led to the founding of a number of networks led by young men like me, most of whom were friends and acquaintances and whom the Enemy baited with lust.

For example, a young church-planter who had planted a church in Southern California helped launch and direct a well-known network, until a moral failure cost him both his position as senior pastor and his platform. Likewise, a young church-planter in Colorado had helped shape a singles' network, until he too was disqualified for moral failure. Sadly, there's a whole list of other young pastors of a variety of note with similar stories.

Meanwhile, some of the pastors from the original Leadership Network's Young Leaders team had continued together without falling into temptation and have now resurfaced as the Emergent Village Network with Brian McLaren.

During these few years, I spent much less time traveling and more time with my wife at home, playing with my kids, stabilizing our quickly growing church, and cofounding the Acts 29 Church Planting Network (which has, at the time of this writing, started over one hundred churches in eight nations in a five-year period).

Now that the time has come to write, I am presenting this book as a contribution toward the furtherance of the emerging church in the emerging culture. Many of the insights in this book are gleaned from my experiences as a founding pastor, the experiences of the theoreticians I've been privileged to meet, the church planters with whom I've helped launch churches, the thousands of people I've spoken to across the country on the radio, the thousands of conversations I've had with pastors at conferences, and personal meditation on Scripture.

Since the mid-1990s, the conversation among young pastors has evolved from reaching Generation X, to ministering in a postmodern culture, to a more mature and profitable investigation of what a movement of missionaries would look like, missionaries sent not from America to another nation but from

America to *America*. This "reformission" is a radical call to reform the church's traditionally flawed view of missions as something carried out only in foreign lands and to focus instead on the urgent need in our own neighborhoods, which are filled with diverse cultures of Americans who desperately need the gospel of Jesus and life in his church. Most significant, they need a gospel and a church that are faithful both to the scriptural texts and to the cultural contexts of America. The timing of this reformission is critical. George Barna has said, "The first and most important statistic is that there are a *lot* of Americans who don't go to church — and their numbers are increasing. The figure has jumped from just 21 percent of the population in 1991 to 33 percent today. In fact, if all the unchurched people in the U.S. were to establish their own country, they would form the eleventh most populated nation on the planet."[1]

What I am advocating is not an abandonment of missions across the globe but rather an emphasis on missions that begin across the street, like Jesus commanded (Acts 1:8).

Meanwhile, the churches in our neighborhoods may be more akin to museums memorializing a yesterday when God showed up in glory to transform people, than to the pivot points of a movement working to reform the culture of the present day. Reformission requires that we all learn the principles handed down to us from mentors who are seasoned cross-cultural missionary pioneers, such as Lesslie Newbigin, Hudson Taylor, and Roland Allen. These missionaries are most adept at helping us to cross from our church subcultures into the dominant cultures that surround us. Subsequently, at the heart of reformission are clear distinctions between the gospel, the culture, and the church (see figure).[2]

First, the gospel of Jesus Christ is the heart of the Scriptures. To put it succinctly, Paul said that the gospel is of primary importance and consists of Jesus' death, burial, and resurrection to save sinners, in accordance with the Scriptures (1 Cor. 15:1–8).

The Gospel and Our Culture Network's adaptation of Lesslie Newbigin's triangular movement of the gospel*

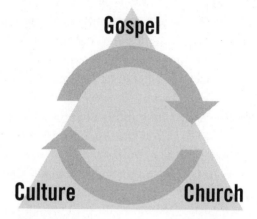

Gospel

Culture　　　　**Church**

* From *The Church between Gospel and Culture*, ed. George Hunsberger (Grand Rapids: Eerdmans, 1996).

Second, we have the various cultures in which people live their lives (for example, ancient Jews and Gentiles; modern, urban homosexual artists; modern, rural heterosexual farmers). Our lives shape, and are shaped by, the culture we live in, and the gospel must be fitted to (not altered for) particular people, times, and circumstances so that evangelism will be effective.

Third, we have the church, or the gathering of God's people — which includes those who are not Christians (Matt. 13:24–30) — where people are built up in their faith and knitted together in loving community. They can then faithfully engage those in the culture with the gospel, while experiencing its transforming power in their own lives.

Reformission is a radical call for Christians and Christian churches to recommit to living and speaking the gospel, and to doing so regardless of the pressures to compromise the truth of the gospel or to conceal its power within the safety of the church. The goal of reformission is to continually unleash the gospel to do its work of reforming dominant cultures and church subcultures.

Reformission therefore begins with a simple return to Jesus, who by grace saves us and sends us into mission. Jesus has called us to (1) the gospel (loving our Lord), (2) the culture (loving our neighbor), and (3) the church (loving our brother). But one of the causes of our failure to fulfill our mission in the American church is that the various Christian traditions are faithful on only one or two of these counts. When we fail to love our Lord, neighbor, and brother simultaneously, we bury our mission in one of three holes: the parachurch, liberalism, or fundamentalism.

Gospel + Culture–Church = *Parachurch*

First, many Christians become so frustrated with the church that they try to bring the gospel into the culture without it. This is commonly referred to as the parachurch, which includes evangelistic ministries such as Young Life and Campus Crusade for Christ. The success of these ministries is due in large part to their involvement in culture and in loving people, whereas the church often functions as an irrelevant subculture. But the failure of such ministries is that they are often disconnected from the local church, connecting unchurched people to Jesus without connecting them to the rest of Jesus' people. This can lead to theological immaturity. Once someone is saved, he or she is encouraged to do little more than get other people saved.

Also, since parachurch ministries are often age-specific, they lack the benefits of a church culture in which all generations are integrated to help people navigate the transitions of life. This further separates families from each other if mom, dad, and kids are each involved in disconnected life-stage ministries outside of their church, rather than in integrated ministries within it.

The parachurch tends to love the Lord and love its neighbors, but not to love its brothers.

Culture + Church–Gospel = *Liberalism*

Second, some churches are so concerned with being culturally relevant that, though they are deeply involved in the culture, they neglect the gospel. They convert people to the church and to good works, but not to Jesus. This is classic liberal Christianity, and it exists largely in the dying mainline churches. The success of these ministries lies in that they are involved in the social and political fabric of their culture, loving people and doing good works. Their failure is that they bring to the culture a false gospel of accommodation, rather than confrontation, by seeking to bless people as they are rather than calling them to a repentant faith that transforms them. Often the motive for this is timidity because, as Paul says, the gospel is foolish and a stumbling block to the unrepentant. Liberal Christians are happy to speak of institutional sin but are reticent to speak of personal sin because they will find themselves at odds with sinners in the culture.

Liberal Christians run the risk of loving their neighbors and their brothers at the expense of loving their Lord.

Church + Gospel–Culture = *Fundamentalism*

Third, some churches are more into their church and its traditions, buildings, and politics than the gospel. Though they know the gospel theologically, they rarely take it out of their church. This is classic fundamentalist Christianity, which flourishes most widely in more independent-minded, Bible-believing churches. The success of these churches lies in that they love the church and often love the people in the church. Their failure is that it is debatable whether they love Jesus and lost people in the culture as much as they love their own church. Pastors at these churches are prone to speak about the needs of the church, focusing on building up its people and keeping them from sinning. These churches exist to bring other Christians in, more than to send them out into the culture with the gospel. Over time, they can become so inwardly focused that the gospel is replaced with rules, legalism, and morality supported with mere prooftexts from the Bible.

Fundamentalist Christians are commonly found to love their Lord and their brothers, but not their neighbors.

Reformission is a gathering of the best aspects of each of these types of Christianity: living in the tension of being Christians and churches who are culturally liberal yet theologically conservative and who are driven by the gospel of grace to love their Lord, brothers, and neighbors. This book focuses on issues related to the scriptural content of the gospel and the cultural context of its ministry, and I write out of my sincere love as a pastor for Christians, churches, lost people, and culture.

In this book, we will examine these themes both theologically and practically. Each chapter is broken into the following sections: First, we will *remember* the teachings of Scripture and examine them for instruction. Second, as an act of correction, we will *repent* of those values, beliefs, and behaviors which are sinful. Third, we will *redeem* our future by obeying God and living by the grace he provides us for action. Fourth, we will *reflect* with God through the study of Scripture, both alone and in community with others.

I invite you to turn the page and begin a radical journey with me as we explore what life in Christ can mean in the context of an emerging church in a changing world. Along the way, I will share insights from my story and from the stories of others.

LOVING YOUR LORD THROUGH THE GOSPEL

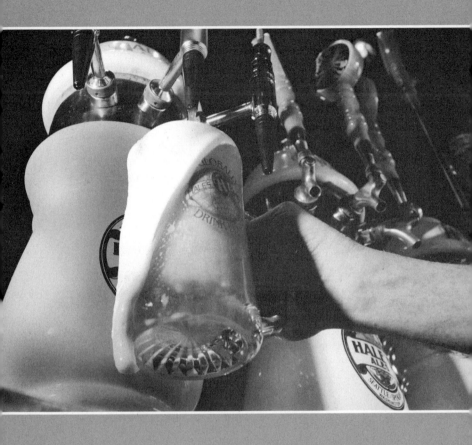

Chapter One

EAT, DRINK, AND BE A MERRY MISSIONARY

Imitating the Reformission of Jesus

Jesus. The first word of this book must be Jesus, because everything, reformission included, begins and ends with him. But the longer someone is a Christian, the greater their propensity to diminish the Jesus of the Bible until he becomes a predictable little God who ceases to surprise them. Therefore, it is imperative that all Christians continually search the Scriptures in order to see Jesus clearly. And as we read of Jesus' involvement in culture, we see a free and radical God whose life is so shocking that it is self-evident that the story is true, because no one in their right mind could make it up. Therefore, to prepare you for reformission, I first want to remind you of the beautifully scandalous life and grace of Jesus Christ.

➲ REMEMBERING:
WHAT GOD'S STORY REVEALS

The story begins with God making all things, then creating a man named Adam. Though Adam is technically perfect, it is still not good for him to be alone. The Bible never tells us why, exactly. Perhaps he would have forgotten to pick up the trash around the Garden of Eden, and the place eventually would have looked like an eternal fraternity without a hint of an annual spring cleaning.

Whatever the case, God creates a perfect woman who is beautiful, sinless, and naked — the same kind of woman every guy ever since has been searching for. Adam meets her and, recognizing that his life has just taken a turn for the better, he sings her a song, after which their marriage is consummated. The Bible could end right there, after only two chapters, with the man and woman naked, eating fruit, and trying to fill the earth all by their happy, horny, holy selves.

But ever since the dreadful day of the Thud in Eden, we have all been walking around scratching our thick skulls, trying to figure out how to get back to that glorious time. Why? Because our happy, naked first parents sinned against God and brought a curse upon themselves and all of creation. They sinned because they believed the lies of a talking serpent who had been an angel until he got kicked out of heaven for his pride.

After they are exiled from Eden, our first parents have two boys, and before long, one boy kills the other. From there, carnage and death ensue, and people grow so wicked that God floods the earth, killing nearly everyone. But he starts over with another decent guy named Noah, who nevertheless ends up having a bad day, gets drunk, and passes out naked in his tent like some redneck on vacation.

As time rolls along, God also works through a cowardly old man named Abraham, who is happy to whore out his loving and beautiful antique of a wife to avoid conflict. God also chooses to work through a guy named Jacob, even though he's a trickster and a con man. Later, God raises up a stuttering murderer named Moses to lead his people. Years later, a king named David comes onto the leadership stage, but he becomes an adulterer, a murderer, and an odd type pointing ahead to the promised Christ. David's son Solomon redefines addiction, with more wine, women, and money than any guy could possibly know what to do with, though he gave it a good Hefner-esque run. This brief list doesn't even include the prophets, like Ezekiel, whom God tells to cook a meal over his own feces; Hosea, who marries a prostitute; Jeremiah, who cries like a newly crowned beauty queen all the time; or any of the freaks on cable television right now talking about *Jee*-zus along with their wives, who by God's grace alone are not naked like their mother Eve.

And to top it all off, God comes to earth. He has a mom whom everyone thinks is a slut, a dad whom they think has the brilliance of a five-watt bulb for believing the "virgin birth" line, and brothers who likely pummel him frequently, because even God would have to get at least one wedgie from his brothers if he were to be fully human. The God-Man goes through puberty and likely goes through that weird vocal transition in which, in the course of one syllable, a young man can seamlessly go from sounding like Barry White to sounding like Cindy Brady. God comes hiding in human flesh and, according to Isaiah the prophet, he's a regular-looking guy. In sum, nobody knows exactly who this guy is.

Doesn't the story sound like the plot of a trashy, daytime television talk show? The God-Man is born to a teenage virgin in an animal stall, grows up with a blue-collar dad in a dumpy rural town, and has a weird cousin named John, who lives in the woods and survives on a steady diet of bugs, sugar, and repentance.

Somehow John becomes the leader of a religious movement with a small posse of guys you'd have to think probably looked like clones of the kid on the porch in the movie *Deliverance*. Then Jesus takes a few of John's posse as his own. At this point in the story, God is thirty years of age and a classic underachiever with no wife, kids, stable career, or even much of a home.

But apparently God is fun to hang with, because he and his posse get invited to a lot of parties, including a wedding, which is basically a week-long wine and dance party celebrating some lucky guy's attempt to get back to Genesis 1 and 2. This would be the first of Jesus' many parties.

The constipated religious leaders of his day accuse him of being a drunkard, a glutton, and a crooked guy who always hangs out with the wrong people: easy girls like Mary, crooked mafia types like Matthew, and the kids in high school who always wear black concert T-shirts, sport greasy male ponytails, and smoke cigarettes just off school property during lunch (Matt. 11:19). To the religious leaders, Jesus is a scandal — his followers are felons — and every time they see Jesus, it agitates them that he is always surrounded by a crowd, telling knock-knock jokes to miscreants who love his sense of humor (because his perfection had to have included comedic timing).

Anyway, Jesus shows up at a wedding and begins his public ministry. God has come to earth, and he kicks things off as a bartender. Some poor kids getting married have run out of wine and face humiliation with their friends and family. So Jesus' mom, Mary, comes and asks her son, God, to do something about it.

In a show of irony, he takes six large stone jars used for ceremonial washing and asks for them to be filled with water, not for cleansing and religious purification but so he can turn that water into wine. And this is not the cheap wine named after a bird or a handgun but good wine, fine wine, the kind bearing a foreign name most Americans can't even pronounce because it is not spelled B-u-d-w-e-i-s-e-r.

The Bible says that this is how the sovereign, eternal God of the universe first makes his glory known. Paul says this message of Jesus sounds like foolishness and that many people trip over him in their failed attempts to find him. Why? The reasons are legion, but they include the ignorance of the freedom *of* Christ from which Christians obtain their freedom *in* Christ. In an effort to illustrate this truth, I will tell you about an experience I had with a gay cowboy friend of mine.

⟳ REPENTING:
WHAT HAPPENED IN A BAR

As a newer Christian, I was the plankton in a conservative, sub-urban megachurch food chain. My hope was to get called up to the big leagues and be a full-time pastor, and so I attended a solid Bible-teaching seminary, volunteered at the church, and labored to build a good reputation as a morally upright man. I did not drink, smoke, or do anything that could give others the impression that I was a *bad* sinner.

Then I got a phone call from an old college friend whom God had used to bring me to faith. He was a zealous charismaniac type who had relentlessly chased me around campus the first few months of my freshman year, trying to get me to pray the Sinner's Prayer. After my conversion, he became a Christian friend. But in the years since college, I had lost touch with him. So I was now happy to hear his voice on the phone, and we scheduled a time to get together.

Over lunch, he informed me that he had been a closet homo-sexual throughout college, had joined the military after graduation, and had recently been discharged for having sex with fellow soldiers. He was presently frequenting public bathrooms throughout the city and having anonymous sex with various men. He shared that he was wrestling through whether he believed that he was a sinner and whether he still believed in God. When I invited him to attend church with me, he declined, saying that it was unfair for me to expect him to come into my Christian subculture, since I was unwilling to go with him into his homosexual subculture.

And he was right. So, feeling convicted to be like Jesus, I told him I would be happy to go into his world if he would come into mine. Seeing an evil dervish grin emerge on his face, I knew I was in trouble. He invited me to a gay country and western bar he frequented. At the time, I did not drink and disliked no one more than limp-wristed gay men and cowboys. I could not conceive of a worse purgatory than the one awaiting me.

I went home to inform my lovely bride about the mess I had gotten myself into, discovering that she was both supportive and good humored. The following week, I went out with my skinny, feminine gay buddy, who was dressed up in tight jeans, goofy boots, and a big hat for a night of country line-dancing. Walking through the front door of the queer cowboy club, I was hit with the shrill sound of country and western music and the sight of a sea of skinny men sporting tight jeans, well-groomed mustaches, and boots, even though we were in the middle of downtown Seattle and at least an hour's drive away from the nearest horse.

My friend took me to the bar and introduced me to a number of his gay buddies, who were drinking — of course — light beer. Feeling like I was wearing someone else's underwear, I stood there and tried to be inconspicuous, praying that no one would recognize me. Then someone I had graduated from high school with approached me with a surprised look. She asked, "What are you doing here?" And I quickly blurted, "I'm married to a woman and here with a friend, but I'm not a gay guy, so please don't tell anyone I'm a queer." She laughed and we chatted for a few minutes until a song she obviously liked came on, and she then shuffled off to the dance floor with her girlfriend.

Then a guy introduced himself and hit on me. Stunned, I did not immediately respond but instead stared at the poor guy, trying to figure out why he looked so familiar, how he could mistake me for a gay guy, and if I was really good looking. It then hit me and I asked him, "Are you my mailman?" He replied, "Yes, I am a mailman." Suddenly, I wanted to kill myself and never get mail again.

My buddy had abandoned me at the bar, and I frantically searched for him in hopes that if I was with him, no one else would hit on me. I found him drinking a fruity drink and flirting with an enormous man. I asked him how long we were staying, since the first five minutes in this hell were about all I could handle. But he said, "Mark, I have to go to a special room upstairs for about an hour, so you are welcome to come up with me or stay down here until I return." I asked what they did in that room, hoping I would not throw up my dinner after hearing his answer. Here's how he responded: "It's not an orgy. It's a meeting for the gay rodeo committee."

Gay rodeo?

Those were simply the last two words I had ever anticipated hearing together. He explained that the queer cowboys were hoping to have a rodeo and that he was on the planning committee. Not wanting to sit at the bar for an hour getting hit on, I chose to go to the planning meeting with a few dozen other guys. We all sat in a circle like we were in a home Bible study. The meeting opened with introductions, everyone giving their names and vocations.

I had prided myself on aspiring to the pastorate but now found myself in an awkward position. My buddy leaned over and whispered in my ear, "What are you going to tell them you do for a living?" Unsure, I said, "I have no idea. Maybe I'll tell them I am a teacher or a spiritual director."

When it came to my turn, I tried to avoid the inevitable conflict and lied to them by saying I was a spiritual something-or-other, hoping the queer cowboys would smile, nod, and ignore me. But one of the cowboys asked what my religion was. So I came out of my closet and told him I was a Bible-thumping, old-school Christian preacher, causing some of the guys to laugh, thinking I was kidding. The rest of the meeting went well and was not all that different from the boring staff meetings we had at the mega-church, where people who hadn't done much tried to appear as if they had. The guys were very nice, so afterward when we returned downstairs, I ended up buying some of them beers. However, I did not drink that evening because I wanted to respect the church's authority over me, which forbade alcohol consumption.

One of the guys asked if I was actually a real pastor and began explaining how his lover and many of his friends had died of AIDS. Actually, he began discipling me, articulating with great pain the loneliness and death that filled his community and explaining why he feared death. He asked what happens when someone dies and wanted to know what would happen to him, in particular. He was attentive as I sought to relate the gospel to his life: sin causes death, but Jesus is God who became a man and died — when he was about the same age as this man — in order to rise from death, forgive sin, and give eternal life to those who repent of sin and trust in him. I explained that only Jesus can take us through our own deaths and comfort us after the deaths of others, because he alone has been through death and come back.

The man was not converted during our chat, but in many ways, I was.

As I left the bar, God convicted me about my proud addiction to morality and my attempt to look like a decent guy so that others would like me. I was so insecure that I feared not only that my Christian friends would see me walking out of a gay bar with queer cowboys but also that the queer cowboys would reject me for being a Bible thumper who, deep down, believed they were running headlong to hell in their cowboy boots. I cared more about how I appeared to people than about whether I shared the passion of Jesus for those who are lost.

That night, I learned that reformission requires that Christians and their churches move forward on their knees, continually confessing their addictions to morality and the appearance of godliness, which does not penetrate the heart and transform lives. In the end, I learned that God's mission is not to create a team of moral and decent people but rather to create a movement of holy loving missionaries who are comfortable and truthful around lost sinners and who, in this way, look more like Jesus than most of his pastors do.

⟳ REDEEMING:
WHAT IT MEANS TO CROSS BARRIERS

Driving home from the gay cowboy bar with my buddy, it hit me that I had just spent an evening in Samaria. In Jesus' day, what we now refer to as the Holy Land was divided into three regions. In the north was Galilee, in the south was Judea, and in the middle was Samaria. Samaria was the ghetto, where all the unclean and undesirable mixed-race people, with their convoluted Oprah-esque mixed religion, lived.

What's our modern-day equivalent to Samaria? Could it be Salt Lake City, Utah, which is filled with people who claim to worship Jesus but who have their own religion, complete with their own temple and sacred underpants?

In Jesus' day, the tension between Samaritans and Jews was intense. The Samaritans still claimed to believe in the first five books of the Old Testament, though they had cut themselves off from the riches of the rest of the Old Testament; they claimed to be children of Abraham, though they continued as a blended religion filled with pagan and occultic beliefs and practices. The Jews were so disgusted by the Samaritans that they rarely traveled through their land. When they did, it was not uncommon for Jews to be detained and harassed merely for traveling through Samaria.

When Jesus relocated his ministry to Galilee, he chose to travel through Samaria, rather than avoiding that region. On his way, he sat down at Jacob's well for a rest while his disciples went to town to buy lunch. As he rested, a Samaritan woman came to the well to draw water. We do not know her name; we do, however, know her reputation. She was the dirty, leathery faced town whore. After a string of five failed marriages, she had resorted to shacking up with a man with whom she traded sex for rent.

She did not say a word to Jesus, likely because she guessed that a Jewish rabbi was not interested in chitchat with a woman like her. She arrived at the well alone in the heat of midday, because she knew that the reputable women who had gathered earlier in the cool of the day to draw water and to gossip would have welcomed her about as warmly as the KKK would have greeted Malcolm X at a Klan rally.

The story takes a surprising twist when Jesus spoke kindly to her, asking, "Will you give me a drink?" Stunned, the woman likely scrunched up her nose and stared at Jesus in bewilderment, because in that cultural setting, men did not befriend women, Jews did not befriend Samaritans, and upright rabbis did not befriend crooked sinners. But Jesus is holy, which simply means he is different without being sinful, and so he spoke to her kindly, asking her a favor and treating her as a friend.

Travelers in that day usually carried a container for water, and Jesus' men had apparently taken theirs into town, leaving him with nothing to drink. So Jesus requested a drink from her container. This act of drinking from her vessel would likely have been viewed as sinful, dirty, and ritually unclean by the Jews. So his request, while not in violation of Scripture, trampled religious moral dogma.

A master teacher, Jesus used the metaphor of water to speak to the woman about salvation — or cleansing living water — given by God. In a clever attempt to expose her sin and her need for God's forgiveness, Jesus requested that she first go home to get her husband before he would give her living water. She replied with a half-truth, that she had no husband. Jesus then named her sin, saying he knew that she had been married five times and was now living in sin with a man who was not her husband.

The naming of the woman's sin was the turning point in the conversation, as the woman then recognized Jesus as a prophet deserving respect, so she referred to him as "sir." This would have been appropriate, since the Samaritans were waiting not for a Messiah but instead for the promised prophet who would be like Moses.

The woman asked Jesus about the theological issue dividing their religions, races, and worship. Where should she go to confess her sin and be reconciled to God? Should she go to her Samaritan temple on nearby Mount Gerizim, or should she travel to the temple in Jerusalem?

Jesus' answer was nothing less than the first shot in a revolution that has continued ever since. In his simple answer, he declared an end to both Samaritan and Jewish worship in favor of worship that requires not just outward tradition and ritual but, more important, inward spirit and truth to please God. Jesus declared that the Father was actively seeking worshipers and that he would give people the truth by sending the Holy Spirit to teach them whom to worship. Because of the Spirit, people would no longer need to go to any sacred place such as a temple. Instead, we can worship God anywhere and everywhere, if we turn from sin to receive the Spirit, who would dwell in us, thereby making our bodies (including the body of this woman, who likely smelled like cheap liquor and men at that very moment) into a new temple where the presence of God dwells.[1]

The word Jesus tenderly used for worship literally means "to kiss toward." In Jesus, God had just blown this haggard harlot a metaphorical kiss of loving grace and had proposed a covenant of love that, unlike all the others she had experienced, would endure. Predictably, the woman was so stunned that she sobered up. With her heart now yearning for forgiveness and under-standing, she told Jesus that she longed for the day when God would come as the Messiah-Christ and explain all of these things to her. Peering into her tearful eyes, and likely leaving a painful silence before speaking, Jesus simply declared, "I who speak to you am he."

Lest we overlook the magnitude of this moment, notice that this is the only place in John's gospel that Jesus declares that he is the promised Old Testament Messiah. And he reserved this great revelation not for the seminary professors or megachurch senior pastors but for the woman he had come to earth to spir-itually court at a lonely well in the heat of the noontime sun. And Jesus revealed her sin, putting his finger on the dirtiest and most scarred portion of her soul, which smelled like death, hell, and sin. He cleaned it, healed it, forgave it, and replaced it with grace and the Holy Spirit, as only he can.

Born again, the woman decided to start her life over, which is the essence of repentance. She sprinted back into Sychar with good news to tell. She told anyone who would listen that she had been a sick and wicked woman governed by her loneliness and perversion but that things had changed once she met Jesus. We can only imagine the looks on people's faces, including the many men who likely had seen her unclothed but who had never seen her clothed in righteousness. As the first evangelist in the New Testament, she was doing the work of mission in her culture, pointing others to Jesus for salvation and life.

Many heretical, outcast idolators came to believe in Jesus because of this woman's testimony. They correctly saw him as Savior for all nations of the earth because of one changed life. They then invited Jesus to join them as friends in sinful Sychar. So he remained with them for two days, teaching and seeing many more people believe.

It is likely that John's account gives just the highlights of a lengthy conversation that Jesus had with the woman. But it illustrates Jesus' bold crossing of the barriers that had separated people from God. Jesus overcame the racial barrier between Jews and Samaritans to show that though the message of salvation came from God through the Jews, it was ultimately intended for all nations of the earth. Jesus overcame the sin barrier and exposed the habitual sexual sin of the woman as the reason she had been unable to worship. Jesus overcame the gender barrier and showed God's gracious heart for this woman and for all women. Jesus overcame the geographical barrier and opened the possibility that everyone everywhere could worship if they would repent of sin, because the Father was seeking them and would give them the truth and the Spirit.

And in his greatest act of love for this woman, Jesus later hung on a Roman cross — punished between two thieves — dying for the many sins of this woman. Jesus then rose from death and ascended into heaven to prepare an eternal home for her. He then sent the Holy Spirit to empower her new life and ministry.

Reformission is ultimately about being like Jesus, through his empowering grace. One of the underlying keys to reformission is knowing that neither the freedom *of* Christ nor our freedom *in* Christ is intended to permit us to dance as close to sin as possible without crossing the line. But both are intended to permit us to dance as close to sinners as possible by crossing the lines that unnecessarily separate the people God has found from those he is still seeking. To be a Christian, literally, is to be a "little Christ." It is imperative that Christians be like Jesus, by living freely within the culture as missionaries who are as faithful to the Father and his gospel as Jesus was in his own time and place.

I am advocating not sin but freedom. That freedom is denied by many traditions and theological systems because they fear that some people will use their freedom to sin against Christ. But rules, regulations, and the pursuit of outward morality are ultimately incapable of preventing sin. They can only, at best, rearrange the flesh and get people to stop drinking, smoking, and having sex, only to start being proud of their morality. Jesus' love for us and our love for him are, frankly, the only tethers that will keep us from abusing our freedom, yet they will enable us to venture as far into the culture and into relationships with lost people as Jesus did, because we go with him.

So reformission requires that God's people understand their mission with razor-sharp clarity. The mission is to be close to Jesus. This transforms our hearts to love what he loves, hate what he hates, and to pursue relationships with lost people in hopes of connecting with them and, subsequently, connecting them with him. This actually protects us from sin, because the way to avoid sin is not to avoid sinners but to stick close to Jesus.

➲ REFLECTING:
REFORMISSION QUESTIONS

If you have not recently read the account of Jesus and the woman at the well, I would encourage you to read John 4:1–42 and then answer the following questions.

1. Who do some Christians in your town, or the larger area in which you live, consider to be Samaritans? Why do you think some Christians dislike them?

2. What parts of your town or area are like Samaria to you — the places you avoid because you do not like the people who live there?

3. What were the Samaritan woman's sins? What do you think might be some common sins among the Samaritans in your town?

4. What pains must the woman's sins have caused her? What pains are your Samaritans' sins causing them?

5. In your area, where are the Jacob's wells and pagan temples where the Samaritans hang out?

6. What barriers did Jesus need to cross to evangelize the Samaritan woman? What barriers would you need to cross to connect with the Samaritans in your culture?

7. What changes took place in the woman's lifestyle? What might change in the lives of the Samaritans in your town or area if they met Jesus and repented of their sinful lifestyles?

8. Why do you think Jesus' disciples did not say anything when they saw him speaking with the Samaritan woman? What do you think some of your Christian friends might say if you befriended a Samaritan?

9. Why was the woman at the well best suited to do mission to Sychar? Which people, if converted, would be best suited for mission in your town?

10. What was Jesus' sense of urgency for harvesting souls, and do you and your Christian friends share his sense of urgency? Why or why not?

11. In what ways is your salvation story (or perhaps the story of someone you know) similar to the story of the woman at the well?

REFORMISSION INTERVIEW WITH DAVID BRUCE
Hollywood Jesus

1 What is your name?

David Bruce

2. Do you consider yourself to be a Christian?

Yes. My spiritual journey began in North Hollywood, California, where I grew up in a Christian home. I responded to Christ at age nine through baptism. I have always been a follower of Jesus Christ. After working in radio, television, and publishing, I moved to Chicago to attend seminary, where I graduated with an M.Div. degree. I have pastored several churches.

3. What is your age?

55

4. What is your vocation?

I am host of the HollywoodJesus.com website [which has received more than 148 million hits], a church leader, an author, and a speaker. I have always had a deep and abiding interest in both Jesus and film. I have an immense library of books on theology, popular culture, and film, and thousands of videos and DVDs. I love to go to church and to film festivals. For me, they are both spiritual experiences. This continuing interest in culture and Jesus led to the creation of the HollywoodJesus.com website in 1998. Actually, the site resulted from a challenge given by Billy Graham to use the internet for good.

5. How have people responded to your faith and website?

I get scores of e-mails a day from all over the world; about 50 percent are from non-Christians regarding faith issues. It has afforded me the best evangelistic opportunity of my life. God has been so gracious. It has been my pleasure to enter into dialogue and to journey with them.

6. Do you consider yourself a missionary to your culture?

Yes, in the truest sense. The Mars Hill approach of Acts 17 is my model for ministry. Instead of throwing rocks at culture, I build bridges. I use Hollywood films as common ground, just as any missionary would use native stories. I look for redemptive analogies — connecting points to the gospel of Jesus Christ.

7. What insights have you gained that would be helpful to Christians and churches?

The top one hundred films of all time have just one thing in common. They are all about relationship. The same is true of pop music, country and western, novels, and television shows. People respond to relationship; it's what we all seek most. The church can furnish positive and caring relationships and help people come to a personal relationship with God through Jesus Christ. In fact, that is what the church is all about. Instead of throwing rocks at the culture, as the church often does, it needs to build bridges to a hurting world in need of a healing relationship with God. Bottom line: let's find common ground and build bridges to a world that "God so loves."

Chapter Two

AND NOW, THE NEWS

Shaping a Reformission Gospel

A few years ago, a friend kindly invited me to cohost a late-night national radio talk show with him. During the six years that *Street Talk* aired, we spent three hours every Saturday night "giving straight answers to tough questions" from callers in their teens and early twenties who tuned in from across the country. We did not screen our calls, and we promised to answer any question about life and God, which made for wildly unpredictable radio.

For the first few years of the show, the majority of questions were the usual inquiries from struggling and new Christians about such things as the deity of Jesus and the trustworthiness of the Bible. But as the show matured and began airing on some non-Christian stations, the nature of the calls shifted, coming more from a pagan and unchurched audience whose questions were not addressed in the

Christian books on apologetics and evangelism available at the time. The new non-Christian listeners, for example, believed that there is a God, that God answers prayer, and that Jesus existed and performed miracles. Their resistance to Christianity was often not theological but practical; they were concerned that they might have to alter such things as their sex lives and drug use if they converted.

As we answered very frank questions, our audience began growing because people identified with the tough issues we were tackling. Simultaneously, a backlash from Christians began to grow, because many of them did not consider it appropriate to have these conversations on their Christian radio stations.

And then *the* call came in. God had recently saved a young couple who lived in Texas. They had only a very basic understanding of the Bible but sincerely loved Jesus and were earnestly trying to arrange their lives in such a way as to honor him. But one issue had become concerning to them: their pastor and Christian friends had told them that oral sex is a sin. The wife, who called our show, explained that her husband enjoyed her performing oral sex on him and that she enjoyed doing so. She said that they had read the Bible trying to find an answer but did not see any prohibition against it, though their Christian friends were vehement in their assertion that it is evil. She emphasized that they would do whatever the Bible says, but they did not want to stop what they were doing unless it is a sin.

I remember taking a deep breath and looking across the microphone at my friend who hosted the show. We both raised our eyebrows, recognizing the hornets nest we were about to stir up. We could tell the woman the truth and inflame much of our Christian audience, or we could disobey God and keep our radio program on the air. My friend waved toward the microphone, signaling me to answer the question, which I did, taking the woman through the Song of Songs and showing her how the Bible poetically describes the act as a beautiful and enjoyable experience to be shared only by married couples. She and her husband thanked us, and the phone began ringing off the hook with calls from irate Christians accusing us of promoting sodomy and perversion. Within a few days, the outrage grew so intense that some radio stations around the country began dropping us from their programming schedules, despite our excellent ratings. Though we had been faithful to God and to Scripture, we had violated the taboos of a segment of the Christian subculture.

In hindsight, our radio show underwent the same process that the early church had. As the gospel jumped from the Jewish culture to the unreached Gentile culture, a rigorous debate followed in an effort to sort out what is gospel, what is sin, and what is simply baggage the sending culture had added to the gospel like barnacles that attach to a boat as it sits tied to a dock. In the apostle Paul's day, these controversial issues included the eating of meat sacrificed to idols, the proper day of worship, circumcision, dietary restrictions, cursing, holidays, and sexual activities.[1] These were not widely debated or controversial issues within Judaism, since the Jews had settled these matters within their own culture. But when the gospel moved into Gentile cultures, commonly held assumptions were suddenly called into question, which upset many Jewish Christians who believed that people from other cultures should convert to both Jesus and their culture. Likewise, as the gospel moves into new cultures in our day, and as new cultures emerge, we must struggle to sift out what is cultural and what is scriptural.

➲ REMEMBERING:
SIFTING CULTURAL FROM SCRIPTURAL

For example, as a pastor in Seattle, I have fielded the following difficult cultural questions that probably had not been widely debated before in the history of the Christian faith. You may find them offensive, but recognize that these are questions that some people today are asking, whether we're ready to hear them or not:

- Can I pierce any part of my body in an attempt to look like a spinning rack displaying fishing lures at a tackle shop?
- Can I tattoo the body God has given me?
- If I am an HIV-positive new Christian, can I still get married someday?
- Can I get a sex change because I feel like God made me the wrong gender?
- Can I get breast implants as my husband's Christmas gift?
- What words count as swearing, who decides this, and if I disagree, can I cuss them out?
- Can I continue to make a living by being a professional blackjack player now that I am a Christian?
- Is it okay for a woman to look like a man, or a man to look like a woman?
- Is it okay to improve my appearance with plastic surgery?
- Does a wife really need to submit to her husband, or is this an outdated practice of a long-forgotten culture in which people were happily married for longer than it took to grow a beard?
- Is it a sin to use birth control or to get a vasectomy to prevent pregnancy?
- Are there any sexual practices between a husband and wife that are outlawed in the Scriptures?
- Why are smoking cigarettes, drinking coffee, or taking prescription mood-altering medications okay, but smoking pot is considered a sin?

- How can masturbation be a sin if it's never mentioned in the Bible?
- Can a woman be a pastor?
- Is homosexuality always a sin, or can a loving and monogamous same-sex couple remain together if they become Christians?
- If a married couple videotapes their lovemaking solely for their own viewing pleasure, is this a sin?

The salvation of the Gentiles in my town, like the salvation of the Gentiles in the New Testament, raises a host of theological questions that desperately need to be answered. As a pastor, I have frequently been asked each of the questions listed above and have had to provide thoughtful and biblical answers. They were asked by sincere new Christians who had no church background and wanted to know whether the things they were doing were sins to repent of or matters of freedom. Reformission is about the old gospel answering without blushing the new questions that emerge from new cultures.

➲ REPENTING:
NOSTALGIA AND INNOVATION

For some Christians, however, the pace and types of change in their culture, combined with the types of questions and sins that ensue, are nothing short of frustrating. Why? Partly because people are prone to live either in the past or in the future, while neglecting the present. Christians, however, are supposed to live today, in light of yesterday, for the sake of tomorrow. Therefore, shouldn't the propensity for either nostalgia or innovation be repented of as sin?

Arguably, most Christians and churches prefer the past to the present or the future, because the past is over, while the present and the future still require a lot of work. A naive romanticism in each of us desperately wants to believe there was a time after

Genesis 2 when the world was a wonderful place to live, when things were better and easier than they are today. This powerful delusion enables us to excuse our laziness and failure to be about reformission because of the difficult days we live in. No wonder many denominations and theological traditions continually speak more of the days past when their movement began than of the present days that are upon them and the future days into which they are moving.

For example, a pastor friend of mine was hired by a dying church. At one time, the church's enormous facility had housed nearly nine thousand people, but the congregation had dwindled over the years to roughly one hundred, most of whom were beyond retirement age. They hired him in hopes of keeping their church from joining the more than three thousand churches in the United States that die each year. What he quickly learned, however, was that while they wanted things to change, *they* did not want to change. To this day, they remain unwilling to change the aesthetics of their very dated sanctuary, or to upgrade their sound system, which is nearly thirty years old, or to reconsider the style of their worship music, or to make any adjustments to their programming or philosophy of ministry.

Decades ago, these people had successfully practiced mission and brought the gospel to their culture because they were simultaneously faithful to the content of Scripture and to the context of ministry. But as the times changed, they did not, preferring to speak nostalgically of a time when they were successful. They long for a return to the day when people walked to church, preferred an organ to a band, and were loyal to the denominational traditions of their parents.

This propensity among God's people to be nostalgic is nothing new. After the more than four hundred years of the Israelites' brutal slavery to Egyptian pharaohs, God liberated his people. But they soon began reminiscing about the "good old days" when they were slaves, and they longed to return to the past. However foolish this may seem, nostalgia remains perennially popular.

Perhaps Solomon said it best: "Do not say, 'Why were the old days better than these?' For it is not wise to ask such questions" (Eccl. 7:10). There has never been a "good old day" since the Great Thud in Eden. Every age is filled with sin, sinners, God's love, and work to be done. Each generation has its resistance to the gospel, and each culture is equally far from God because of sin and equally close to God because of his love. As Solomon repeatedly says, there is indeed nothing new under the sun.

At its best, a sense of tradition informed by a grasp of the successes and failures of Christians who have gone before us is vital today. At its worst, traditionalism fails to distinguish between biblical principles for ministry and cultural methods for implementing those principles. Traditionalism clings to dated ineffective methods in the name of staying truer to tradition than to Scripture.

The result of traditionalism is a Christianity that has all of the right answers to all of the wrong questions, because the questions that were once pressing are no longer being asked. The dying church I mentioned desired to attract the multitude of non-Christians who lived close to them, so they hosted a debate between an atheist and a Christian. They went to great expense only to have no one from the community attend. Why? Because the church did not know that atheism, popular a generation or two ago, is virtually dead today. This church believed that people are either Christians or atheists, and because they didn't know their neighbors, they wrongly assumed that, since their neighbors were not Christians, they must be atheists. Actually, their neighbors were very spiritual people who spent great amounts of time praying but had no idea to whom.

Today's danger is not only nostalgia. Equally damaging to reformission is the tendency, most common among young Christians frustrated with the constraints and failures of backward-looking churches and ministries, to ignore church history and its lessons in pursuit of unrestrained and undiscerning innovation. The irony of this innovation is that churches and ministries that pursue it become so relevant to the culture that they are, in fact, irrelevant and are unable to call lost people from or to anything because they have lost the distinctive and countercultural nature of the gospel. Unrestrained and undiscerning innovation not only contextualizes the gospel to fit a culture but also capitulates it to a culture. This is akin to the behavior of the Israelites, who were prone not only to buddy up with pagan neighbors but also to worship their gods, have sex at their sacred places, and dance around their golden calves.

I recall a terse conversation I had with a very successful and well-known young pastor who desired to reach the many gay, lesbian, and transgendered people living in his urban area. He explained that to do so, he had appointed to his church's leadership someone who had been born a man but was undergoing a sex change operation to become a woman and was living with a male lover. He explained that by elevating this person into a position of leadership, he had won approval from the gay, lesbian, and transgendered community and that this person was greatly helping the people in his church to become more accepting of people like him-her.

Some other pastors and I confronted the young pastor on this matter and told him that, while we agreed that such people need Christ and should be welcomed into the church if they are willing to give the gospel of repentance a hearing, they are still sinners acting out their fallen nature. They should be told that a relationship with Jesus would require a lifestyle change. We clarified that God teaches that he has made us male and female and that no matter what a plastic surgeon might do with someone's plumbing, God's selection of gender remains intact. The pastor vehemently disagreed, arguing that he was simply being relevant to his culture, while we argued, to no avail, that he needed also to be faithful to his God.

Innovation, when not tethered to the truth of the gospel, leads to heresy. Every heretic in the history of the church who took relevance to the culture beyond the bounds of orthodoxy did what Paul, in the opening chapter of Romans, calls exchanging the truth of God for a lie. Paul argues that the true motive inspiring such heretics is that they are either sinning or want to be sinning, and so they suppress the truth like a teenage boy frantically trying to hide his porn magazine when his mom walks into the room.

Whatever happened to that pastor? Eventually he was fired for habitual sexual sin, as he too became so much like the culture in which he lived that in his relevance he became irrelevant and in his innovation he became a heretic.

The underlying motivations for both traditionalism and innovation are a sense of homelessness and a sense of lostness. In our fast-paced and ever-changing culture of insanity, many Christians are prone either to cling to yesterday or to run headlong into tomorrow searching for a home. What's our goal? Not to perpetuate a tradition or embrace an innovation. The goal of reformission is Jesus, to faithfully walk with him on each step of our journey as we head toward the home he has prepared for us. Anything and everything less than life in him, ministry through him, glory to him, by grace from him as we journey with him must continually be repented of as sin, regardless of our history or degree of hipness.

➲ REDEEMING:
THE LANGUAGE OF OUR CULTURE

Once we have cleansed the gospel from the stains of traditionalism and innovation, we are ready to contextualize it in a way that is faithful both to the content of Scripture and the context of ministry. The gospel was meant to live here on the earth among cultures, just as Jesus did during his incarnation. Reformission requires that we carefully express the truth of the gospel in the languages and cultures of the people whom God has called us to evangelize.

Since every presentation of the gospel is culturally expressed, the form of its presentation must continually change as the culture changes, while the content of the gospel remains unchanged and truthful. For example, Billy Graham's booklet *Steps to Peace with God* presents the gospel in terms of peace. It was designed for people who had suffered through a horrendous World War and were desperately longing for peace. God has used it in the lives of many thousands of people in past years. But younger people who have never experienced the horrors of a war like the World Wars and Vietnam are less likely than their parents and grandparents to identify with the thrust of a gospel of peace.

Likewise, the late Bill Bright's Campus Crusade for Christ presentation of the four spiritual laws explains the gospel in terms of four laws that regulate the spiritual world in the same way that four laws govern the physical world, according to Newtonian physics. But younger generations familiar with quantum physics and chaos theory are increasingly less likely to agree with the finality of Newtonian physics or natural laws. They are therefore less likely to relate to a gospel presentation of spiritual laws.

Sometimes you hear the gospel presented in terms of a private religious experience and a loving personal relationship with Jesus. This approach to the gospel made sense to a countercultural hippie generation that had abandoned traditional institutions and authorities (such as the church) in favor of direct and unmediated encounters with God through everything from alternative religions to drug use. But younger people from broken homes in a shattered lonely society desire a community of faith in which to journey and are less likely to see the appeal in an autonomous faith. In addition, people who were raised apart from the church often have less resistance to ancient traditions and institutions. These are foreign experiences that intrigue them, rather than bad memories that repel them.

I don't mean to criticize godly people who have been used of God to bring many to faith. In fact, I have a great deal of respect and appreciation for these people. For example, as a new Christian working at a hotel, I once had the privilege of chatting for about ten minutes with Dr. Billy Graham, who was staying there as a guest. He was sitting in the restaurant by himself, wearing a Minnesota Twins baseball cap, reading the paper, and eating breakfast when I introduced myself. He asked if I knew the Lord, and I explained that I was a new Christian and that God had called me into ministry. His words were encouraging, and he kindly promised to pray for me. After our conversation ended, other people seated around him in the restaurant recognized who he was, and rather than rushing off to avoid being bothered, Dr. Graham graciously stayed in the restaurant to visit with people, share the gospel, and pray over the children who came to sit on his lap and have their photos taken with him as if he were Santa Claus. His gracious spirit and humble approachability made a great impression on many of the non-Christians I worked with. To this day, I sincerely thank God for working through Billy Graham in such a wonderfully faithful manner, both in and out of the pulpit.

Rather than critiquing the methods of men like Dr. Graham, I am simply saying that we should follow their example and be faithful in our own day. Since the gospel must be contextualized in a way that is accessible to the culture and faithful to the

Scriptures, God's people must continually review their presentation of the gospel to ensure that the form in which they present it is the most effective one.

Isn't the way God has chosen to put our Bible together the perfect example of how this is to be done? In the days of the early church, many cultures needed to hear about Jesus in a way they could relate to. So God inspired the writing of four gospels, each designed to present the gospel in the most effective manner to four different cultural groups. This was done without changing the gospel message of Jesus as God, who lived a sinless life, died as a substitute for his people, was buried, and rose from death to forgive repentant sinners according to the promises of Scripture.

Let's do a quick overview of what's distinctive about each gospel:

	Matthew	Mark	Luke	John
Author	Jewish Christian; former despised tax collector	Jewish Christian; cousin of Barnabas	Gentile Christian doctor	Jewish Christian and Jesus' youngest disciple
Primary Audience	Jews	Romans	Gentiles	Greeks
Portrait of Jesus	Jewish Messiah and king	Faithful servant	Perfect man	God
Jesus' Genealogy	Traced to Abraham and David, showing Jesus as the fulfillment of Old Testament prophecy	No genealogy, since Jesus' accomplishments, and not his family, are what is important	Traced to Adam to show that Jesus was fully human	Jesus as the eternal Word of God

Notable Features	Roughly 60% of the book is Jesus' words from his teaching as a rabbi; about fifty Old Testament quotes	Briefest gospel; few Old Testament quotes; explains Jewish words and customs for non-Jews; 150 present-tense verbs emphasizing Jesus' actions; thirty-five miracles, 40% of the book is Jesus' words	Roughly 50% of the book is Jesus' words; thirteen women mentioned that are omitted from other gospels; Jewish customs explained; a focus on Jesus' early years and emotional life	Roughly 90% is unique to John; no parables or exorcisms; seven "I AM" statements of Jesus prove he is God

The way the Gospels in our Bible have been arranged provides a perfect example of how the same gospel story can be presented in different ways. Some critics of Scripture have argued that the differences between the Gospels are contradictions. This could not be farther from the truth. The four gospels simply are similar to your local nightly news. The first three gospels are like local network television affiliates for ABC, NBC, and CBS, which generally report the same stories with some variation in eyewitness accounts and details. This explains why roughly 60 percent of the first three gospels give the same information. John, on the other hand, is more like one of the national cable television newscasts — such as CNN — which have news stories that are rarely found on the local nightly news. This explains why roughly 90 percent of John is unique to his account.

As God's people on reformission, we too are to function as reporters, telling the good news about Jesus in a way that is both scripturally accurate and culturally accessible. So it is vital that we continually look for ways of presenting the gospel that will be best suited for the people we encounter so that they can journey toward Jesus. To help people on this journey, I've found it useful to provide them with certain signposts. Signposts, of course, can be very helpful in giving people directions. We used to live on one of the busiest streets in our city, right next door to the seventy-thousand-seat college football stadium. Giving directions to our home was incredibly easy since the city is filled with signposts directing people to the stadium. But after we became weary of the continual noise and traffic, we purchased a new home in the quietest and most tucked away neighborhood we could find. The only problem was that our dead-end lane was so private that it did not even have a name, which made it nearly impossible to give directions to friends and family members. In addition, none of the internet mapping websites was able to provide accurate directions to our home. So we had to resort to customizing the directions for our guests and carefully explaining which signposts would direct them to our home. Likewise, the cultures that surround you are filled with lost people who cannot find Jesus unless you give them directions with signposts to guide them. I've found the following signposts to be particularly helpful for directing people to Jesus, and I offer them in hopes that you will find them helpful too.

SIGNPOST 1: THE GOSPEL CONNECTS TO THIS LIFE

While previous generations worried about what would happen to them after they died, and were compelled by the idea of belonging to Jesus for the benefits in the life to come, many people today plan on living long but miserable lives and are likely to be more compelled by the idea of belonging to Jesus for the benefits in this life. After all, even if there were no life after death, the joys of belonging to Jesus during this life would, by themselves, make it worthwhile to be a Christian.

AND NOW, THE NEWS • 61

SIGNPOST 2: THE GOSPEL INFUSES DAILY ACTIVITIES WITH MEANING

Every day, people eat, sleep, work, play, love, and hate, but they do not know why. Not knowing where they come from or to whom they are going, they lack the ability to make their lives meaningful. Consequently, our culture is filled with "successful" people who are mired in anxiety and confusion because they do not know the point of all their toil. But the gospel reveals Jesus as Lord over all of life, who infuses even mundane tasks such as dishwashing with meaning as acts of worship.

SIGNPOST 3: THE GOSPEL NAMES SIN AND POINTS THE WAY TO FORGIVENESS

No matter how strenuously people fight them, their consciences prevail in revealing the filthiness of what they have done to others and of what others have done to them. This, in part, explains the explosion in popularity of everything from medication to therapy to make people feel better. Only the gospel can show people not only how bad sin truly is but also the justice of God through Jesus' death in our place to forgive our sin. Once forgiven, we can leave sin behind and move on in newness of life.

SIGNPOST 4: THE GOSPEL TRANSFORMS LIFE

The gospel is about the grace of God given to us through Jesus' death and resurrection for our sins. Grace saves us, and grace forgives and cleanses us when we sin. But grace also empowers us to live new and transformed lives of victory over stubborn sin. In this way, the gospel is about life — new life — in Christ. What people long for most is not just a way to cope with who they are and how to manage their sins. They also yearn for new lives as new people, hence the popularity of television makeover shows. However, an internal makeover is possible only by the transforming power of God's grace.

SIGNPOST 5: THE GOSPEL BUILDS A SPIRITUAL FAMILY

One of the prominent metaphors of the church in the New Testament is a household — or an extended family — held together by the blood of Christ. No wonder the New Testament tells Christians to treat one another as brothers and sisters. In our day of devastated families and generational fracturing, churches that operate like loving spiritual families, caring for and correcting one another in love, can be the most convincing proof of the power and benefits of the gospel.

SIGNPOST 6: THE GOSPEL IS ABOUT PARTICIPATION WITH GOD

While it is true that we are saved not by our good works but by the good works of Jesus (Eph. 2:8–9), it is also true that we are saved *to* good works (Eph. 2:10). The gospel is not simply about getting my sins forgiven and then sitting around until I get to heaven or until Jesus returns. The gospel compels us to participate with God in the culture we live in. Any gospel that does not compel us into mission overlooks both the duties and delights of being a Christian.

SIGNPOST 7: THE GOSPEL IS ABOUT JESUS AS THE MEANS AND END OF OUR SALVATION

Simply, Jesus is not a means to things such as wealth, health, heaven, happiness, wisdom, and success in marriage, church, ministry, theology, or politics. Anytime that Jesus is used as a means to an end, a false gospel has been introduced and the thing improperly focused on becomes a false god. To remain on task with reformission, we must continually be about Jesus as the means and end of God's will, and we must both proclaim his truth and live his lifestyle, which is the topic of the next chapter.

➲ REFLECTING:
REFORMISSION QUESTIONS

1. If you were to write a gospel for the people in your culture, where would you start?
2. If you were to write a gospel for the people in your culture, how would you explain sin?
3. If you were to write a gospel for the people in your culture, how would you explain Jesus?
4. If you were to write a gospel for the people in your culture, what about Jesus' life and teaching would they most resonate with and struggle with? Why?
5. Which of the signposts have been most helpful to you personally?

REFORMISSION INTERVIEW WITH ICHABOD CAINE
Christians and Country Music

1. What is your name?

Ichabod Caine

2. Do you consider yourself to be a Christian?

Yes

3. What is your age?

53

4. What is your vocation?

KMPS Morning Man in Seattle (country music with more than thirty-five years in the industry)

5. How have people responded to your faith and vocation?

Christians go "hey cool," and non-Christians have a general respect, and maybe there's a sliver who are hostile to the gospel, but most are encouraging. My challenge is to be careful as to how vocal I am. There's always this thing about they won't let you share your faith, but God oftentimes puts you in a position where you don't have that kind of liberty; I really do. You look at Jesus — he didn't do thirty-minute sermons; he did short encouraging thoughts and he did proverbs and he spoke in parables. So in that sense, I like to think I am doing my part yet staying in the confines of what my gig calls me to be, which is a disc jockey who happens to be a Christian. I don't think you separate the sacred from the secular. It's all sacred. Oftentimes what we think is sacred is not and what we think is secular is not, so in that sense, I think we are really basically clueless.

6. Do you consider yourself a missionary to your culture?

This question is fraught with some guilt because it basically says you have to be out there … God calls us to be in love with Christ, that's the issue. If you're in love with Christ on a daily basis, the rest takes care of itself. The idea of loading you up with how many Christian scalps have you gotten may make someone think, "Oh, I guess I am doing it wrong." If you are in love with Jesus, you don't have to worry about anything else. Jesus said to go make disciples of all nations; he did not say to go save them. There are really two different arenas here, and we get caught up thinking I may not be doing my part. After having said all this, I still answer this question yes.

7. What insights have you gained that would be helpful to Christians and churches?

Be real. Even if they don't agree with you, if you are authentic and you're real, that can't help but have an attraction. And if you think you are really doing something heavyweight for God and you think it's really religious, you are probably totally wrong.

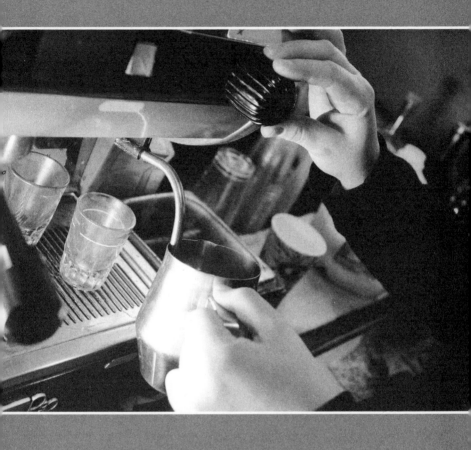

Chapter Three

SHOTGUN WEDDINGS TO JESUS

Reformission Evangelism

⭢ REMEMBERING:
PARTICIPATION

When God called me to plant our church, Mars Hill Church, I had worked for nearly two years overseeing a college ministry, but I had never been a pastor or even been an official member of any church. I was unsure of how to begin a church, and so I simply read the Bible and tried to imitate how Jesus gathered the first workers for his ministry. In the opening chapter of John's gospel, I saw that Jesus began his ministry not with a large crowd, a formal program, or an organized event but rather by informally building friendships with a few men. Once those men trusted him, their friends, family members, and coworkers also became his followers. This simple pattern seemed attainable.

So my wife, Grace, and I began opening our lives and home to practice hospitality and extend friendship to anyone who would accept, and within a short time, the small group meeting in our living room grew to about twenty people. At that time, we moved the weekly congregational gathering into a larger room at a nearby church but continued growing the church by bringing people into our home. This pattern continued for the first years of the church until our house simply could not accommodate the more than sixty people who were in our home each week for Bible studies, meals, meetings, and prayer. By this point, our church had grown to a few hundred people, and it had become obvious that every Christian in our church needed to practice Jesus' pattern.

After some Bible teaching on the principles I write about in this book, people in our church began seeing themselves as missionaries in the culture, building friendships for the purpose of showing and sharing the love of Jesus with lost people. Our church continued to grow, and today it is one of the largest in Seattle, having grown at an average of nearly 60 percent each year since its inception. As our people function as missionaries, evangelism is done by the whole church instead of through the dated evangelistic routine of relying on the ministries of professionals, programs, or large formal events. Reformission requires that every Christian and church realize that missions is about not something they do but something they are. We are all on a mission with Jesus every day, and we are either good missionaries or bad.

In the routine model, there are two options. In the first, a notable speaker is brought in to present the gospel to a large audience and to call them to make a decision for Jesus. In the second, Christians are sent out to ask non-Christians leading questions in an effort to compel them to receive Jesus.

In both options, the emphasis is on eliciting a swift decision for Christ without taking the time to build a friendship. In both versions, those who walk forward, stand up, raise their hand, pray a prayer, sign a card, or indicate by some other means their decisions are deemed converts and told to assimilate into churches. Whether they were truly converted is debatable, and the odds of their assimilating into churches are uncertain, unless they already have trustworthy friendships with someone in a church who can serve as a tour guide, introducing them to the language, values, and systems of the church. While Scripture gives examples of the routine model,[1] the mission model of Jesus may prove to be more faithful to God, more fruitful to lost people, and more appealing to Christians who are otherwise fearful of using drive-by evangelism techniques such as knocking on doors and street witnessing (which can feel a lot like playing Duck, Duck, Damned, a revision of the children's game Duck, Duck, Goose).

While these routine patterns of evangelism have proven fruitful in the past — and remain fruitful in some cultural contexts — their effectiveness is waning in the emerging American culture. There was a time when door-to-door evangelism and door-to-door business sales made sense, because many wives were home all day and husbands came home at night for dinner. This routine is no longer as effective because there are fewer stay-at-home wives and mothers. In addition, people's lives are so filled with entertainment, sales pitches, advertising, self-help seminars, and large emotionally moving events of various sorts that people are often unimpressed by large church events or slick Jesus sales pitches complete with canned leading questions.

In reformission evangelism, people are called to come and see the transformed lives of God's people before they are called to repent of sin and to trust in God.[2] Taking a cue from dating is helpful on this point. If we desire people to be happily married to Jesus as his loving bride, it makes sense to let them go out on

Routine Presentation Evangelism (Believe in Jesus, then belong to the church.)	Reformission Participation Evangelism (Belong to the church, then believe in Jesus.)
Gospel information is presented.	A genuine, spiritual friendship between a Christian and a non-Christian is built.
Hearers are called to make a decision about Jesus.	The non-Christian sees authentic faith and ministry lived openly and participates in it.
If an affirmative decision is made, the person is welcomed into the church.	The gospel is naturally present in word and deed within the friendship.
Then friendship is extended to the person.	The non-Christian's conversion to Jesus follows his or her conversion to Christian friendships and the church.
The convert is trained for service in ministry by being separated from the culture.	The church celebrates the conversion of their friend.

a few dates with him instead of just putting a shotgun to their heads and asking them to hurry up, put on a white dress, and try to look happy for the photos.

Reformission evangelism understands that the transformed lives of people in the church are both the greatest argument for, and the greatest explanation of, the gospel. Therefore, it welcomes non-Christians into the church, not so much through evangelistic programs as through informal relationships like Jesus developed with his first disciples. In our church in Seattle, as lost people become friends with Christians, they often get connected to various ministries (for example, helping to run concerts, helping to guide a rock-climbing expedition, taking a class on biblical marriage, helping to develop a website, joining a Bible study, serving the needy) and participate in them before they possess saving faith. In this way, reformission evangelism depends on friendship and hospitality as conduits for the gospel.

As trust is earned over time, lost people will often speak with their Christian friends about "our church" before they speak about "our God." Often they convert first to the church and friendships with its members, and second to God, whom they meet in their friendships and experiences in the church. For example, a woman in our church who knows that she is not a Christian asked if she could host a Bible study in her home and have someone else teach it, because she enjoyed the people in "our church" so much that she was excited to have them in her home.

Reformission evangelism considers it vital that lost people be brought close enough to witness the natural and practical outworking of the gospel in people's lives. Reformission Christians are not ashamed of the gospel, and they speak about Jesus and pray to him in front of their lost friends as they would around their Christian friends; and their lost friends appreciate their authenticity. Their lost friends are comfortable asking them questions about the Christian life, and these reformission Christians have earned the right to give answers as a result of their friendship and hospitality.

At some point, God may grant saving faith to their lost friends and enable them to pass from death to life, but their salvation is ultimately between them and God, as he alone gives salvation. The precise moment of their conversion is known by God, but it is often unknown to them, because authentic conversion is commonly experienced more as a process than as a single moment. Ultimately, what matters most is not when they meet Jesus but that at some point they begin loving him with new hearts and will continue to do so forever.

One of the most fascinating aspects of reformission evangelism is that lost people actually function as missionaries themselves before their conversion. Lost people commonly speak with lost family and friends of what they are learning about Jesus, even inviting them to church and introducing them to their Christian friends. Hence, reformission evangelism is careful not to sever lost people or new Christians from their tribe of lost friends, because those relationships present further opportunities for evangelism. The only exception would be if those relationships were causing someone to fall back into a habitual sin.

OPPORTUNITIES IN OUR EXPERIENCE ECONOMY

Reformission evangelism, patterned after the example of Jesus, is particularly appropriate for our current economy, in which people live much of their lives pursuing experiences. In their book *The Experience Economy,* James Gilmore and Joseph Pine II trace the transitions our economy has undergone from its original commodity base to the present focus on experiences.[3] To understand our current economy, it is important to view it as a series of layers, as new economies are laid upon the old, that work simultaneously and in conjunction with each other. I will briefly summarize the authors' research, with the addition of an information-economy layer.

Layer 1: Commodities-based economy. In this base level of economy, natural resources are extracted by hand from the earth. If you want a home, you must begin by chopping down a tree, and if you want a cup of coffee, you must grow coffee beans. In this economy, people spend most of their time working the raw materials extracted from creation with their hands. If you want something, you must provide it for yourself.

Layer 2: Goods-based economy. In this next level of economy, you pay someone else to make a commodity into a good. If you want a home, you can buy lumber with which to build one, and if you want a cup of coffee, you can purchase coffee beans. In this economy, people have the luxury of acquiring resources through purchase, trade, and barter because experts in various fields have prepared things for their use.

Layer 3: Services-based economy. In this level of economy, someone else turns a commodity into a good and serves it to you. If you want to buy a home, you can pay people (architects, contractors, interior designers, gardeners, painters) to do the work for you, and if you want a cup of coffee, you can sit in a restaurant while other people do all of the work, from growing coffee beans to bringing a hot cup of decaf to your table. In this economy, people can pay specialists to do various tasks for them.

Layer 4: Information-based economy. In this economy, insight, advice, and counsel that are important to your quality of life — or vital to the improvement of the other economies — are invaluable resources. People in this level of economy value information, in addition to commodities, goods, and services, to the degree that they will pay large sums of money for such things as televisions, radios, newspapers, books, magazines, and the internet. In addition, information is used to teach customers about the values of their business. Examples include coffee shops that inform people of their environmentally safe beans and the philanthropy they undertake with profits.

Layer 5: Experience-based economy. In this highest level of economy, people are not provided with an external commodity or good but are given an experience that provides an internal memory. For example, Starbucks coffee shops include each of the five economic layers and are designed to provide an aesthetic experience that appeals to all of the senses. In Starbucks, the music, the scent of coffee, the flavors, the colors and lighting, the feel of the furniture, the amenities (wireless internet connections, board games, newspapers, magazines), and the sale of products (mugs, tea accessories, seasonal products, home espresso machines) combine to create an experience that is much more complicated than just drinking a cup of coffee. The memory of getting out of the house, conducting business, chatting with a friend, and reading a book by a fire is of great value.

People have always craved experiences, but what sets our time in history apart are the amount of leisure time we have to engage in these experiences, the affordability of technology, and the escalating income and quality of life that make it possible for the masses to experience what only the wealthy could afford in previous centuries. Travel is relatively cheap; multi-million-dollar films can be enjoyed for mere dollars; televisions, DVDs, and home-theater systems are ubiquitous; and personal services are viewed as an entitlement.

However, not all experiences are the same. People in our culture pursue at least three types of experiences.

1. *Observation experiences.* These occur when a person is simply observing an event, such as sitting at home watching a TV show or viewing artwork at a gallery. In worship, this form of experience is common in seeker-sensitive churches where a band performs and the people in the congregation do not sing along but watch the singers as they perform.

2. *Participation experiences.* These require some type of effort for involvement in an experience, such as voting via phone or internet to help select the winner of a reality TV program or taking an art class at a gallery. In worship, this would include congregational singing, clapping, the raising of hands, kneeling, and other expressions of participating in the worship of the church.

3. *Immersion experiences.* These go even further than participation experiences in that the consumer is helping to create the experience rather than observing or participating in someone else's experience, such as video games with multiple players and interactive internet chat rooms. In worship experiences, this would include the same elements of participation experiences but would go even farther by, for example, allowing people, while the sermon is being preached, to paint or draw scenes from the sermon text to be displayed after the service, permitting people to come forward for

communion when they feel prepared, allowing people in the congregation to call out the songs they would like to sing next, or permitting congregants to interrupt the sermon to ask questions of the preacher.

Reformission evangelism to our growing experience economy will require Christians and churches to steep the gospel in the culture with increasing creativity, hospitality, and authenticity. This is necessary because lost people living in an experience-based economy are willing to immerse themselves in the life of a Christian community to experience it for themselves and to see firsthand the experiences of people Jesus has transformed.

THE BENEFITS OF REFORMISSION EVANGELISM

In conclusion, the benefits of reformission evangelism are many, including the following.

- Reformission evangelism blurs the lines between evangelism and discipleship, enabling non-Christians to learn a great deal about Scripture and the Christian life before making a decision for Christ.
- People's conversion to Jesus is also a conversion of their old lifestyles to his mission of reaching lost people. This enables them both to be involved in reformission even before their own conversion — through preexisting relationships with people both outside of and inside of the church — and habituates them if and when they are converted to be about reformission.
- Their conversion is not merely a mental assent to facts they believe but is a conversion of the totality of their lives. This prevents them from being carnal Christians and people who live apart from repentance and holiness, wrongly believing they have been saved because they have a few theological facts in order.

- Reformission insists that evangelism is more about a lifestyle for all of God's people than just a ministry program or department for some of God's people, and that the gospel is made clearest by the honest words and open lives of those who have been transformed by grace.

In theory, reformission evangelism may sound wonderful. But for it to happen in reality, God's people must first admit that their own attitudes often get in the way. It is imperative that Christians develop a habit of confessing and repenting of their self-righteousness, which prohibits this natural progress of the gospel through the culture. In saying this, I recognize that I may sound self-righteous and hypocritically judgmental, and so I will illustrate this point through one of my own sinful experiences.

↻ REPENTING:
SELF-RIGHTEOUSNESS

I wanted to buy diapers.

Just diapers.

It wasn't like I was searching for something rare, like a bald eagle or a literate wrestling fan.

Just diapers.

I desperately needed the diapers because my young daughter had just magically recycled milk into a rainbow of neon colors. As I drove the car, she screamed and cried like a Red Sox fan come World Series time, because she, like a Sox fan, desperately longed for a change.

But we were no longer in our sane city of Seattle. Instead, we were in a parallel universe of heat and grumpy elderly men popping Viagra out of PEZ dispensers like kids on Halloween. This culture resembles hell but goes by the name of South Florida.

Leaving my daughter and wife in the car, I ran into a large grocery store and combed every aisle without finding a single diaper.

Finally, I stopped a young man with a mop and asked him where the diapers were. He said I would have to go to a drug store instead because they did not have any diapers at the grocery store. Amazed both at seeing that some men mop and at the fact that some grocery stores don't have diapers, I ran out and sped to a nearby pharmacy. Upon entering, I was delighted to see a row of diapers stacked to the third heaven. Quickly scanning along the row of diapers, I soon found myself at the end without having found the correct size.

They were all adult diapers!

Shaking my head and staring at the floor, I walked to the counter and asked an old woman in a red vest if they carried any children's diapers.

She said, "No."

No?

As she walked away, I could hear her diaper shuffling. I was so astonished that I nearly needed one off the shelf for myself.

My first thought was that God hated these Floridians and was doubled over in heaven laughing at them. My second thought was that it was only me who hated them and was doubled over laughing at them.

Why?

Because their universe was foreign to me. I did not — could not — understand a childless community where wealthy eighty-year-old men trade in their eighty-year-old wives for four twenty-year-old girlfriends who change their diapers for them. Upon returning to the car, I told my wife that I was grateful that God had not sent me into ministry in South Florida, because wealthy old people are like kryptonite to me.

While I know that our pluralistic and multicultural society frowns on prejudice, the fact remains that we all have prejudices. The more I read the Bible, the more I am convicted of my dislike of some people and of my arrogant self-righteousness. To illustrate my point, I will share with you some of the people whom I had sinful attitudes against that I had to repent of.

I used to dislike men with ridiculously hairy ears and noses, because it looks like they snorted a cat, and I hate cats.

I used to dislike men who wore tank tops, because they remind me of Detroit, and I don't like Detroit because it is a third-world city where a lot of people wear tank tops.

I used to not like Canada, because it is filled with Canadians, and Canadians are hockey fans, and hockey is dumb because it claims to be a sport but does not even have a ball or a pitcher.

I used to not like people who wear white shoes or socks with dark-colored pants, because they look like they are attending a formal event in Canada or Detroit.

I used to dislike minivans, because they are the product of a vast feminist conspiracy to inflict a dignity vasectomy upon men.

I used to dislike men who wear pastel colors, because it is impossible to be masculine wearing turquoise, sea-foam green, lemon yellow, or peach, and these colors are often worn by boy bands, and I despise boy bands because they are happy, they dance, and they encourage teenage girls to gather in groups and scream.

I used to not like people who eat lots of foods that end in "-itos," listen to country music, or refer to Jesus, Elvis, and Dale Jarrett as the Holy Trinity, so I was prejudiced against most of the Deep South.

I used to not like people who wear a mullet (a haircut prevalent at state fairs, NASCAR races, and wrestling matches that is long in the back and short in the front. It is also referred to as the Soccer Rocker, Camaro Cut, Tennessee Mudflap, Kentucky Waterfall, Ape Drape, Achey Breaky Bad Mistakey, Beaver Paddle, Canadian Passsport, Crazy Charismatic Coiffure, and Hockey Hair), because they look like one of the guys in the middle of the evolutionary chart and remind me of my photo in my late-1980s high-school yearbook.

I know this all sounds terrible, and it is. But I'd appreciate your being honest also and admitting that you too have your list of people whom you dislike. You probably think your list is better than mine because it has abortion doctors, rapists, pedophiles, corporate thieves, used-car salesmen, politicians, and evil dictators on it. But the fact that we each have a list means that we are all pretty much the same and are just haggling over the details of who should wear the white hats and who should wear the black. This also helps explain the finger-pointing both in the church and in the culture between blacks and whites, young and old, rich and poor, ugly and beautiful, smart and dumb, urban and rural, self-help and self-acceptance, victims and perpetrators, Republicans and Democrats, Chevy and Ford, Mac and PC, married and single, homosexual and heterosexual, male and female, and educated and uneducated, to name a few. The more we understand the concept of reformission, the more we realize that everyone is unlovely, Jesus loves everyone, and it is his love alone that makes us lovely.

The bottom line is that we are all self-righteous. We are all prone to secretly believe that we are somehow better than others because of things we do or do not do. The Scriptures teach that no one is inherently righteous and that our only righteousness comes from Jesus as a gift.[4] Anyone who fails to embrace this humbling fact invariably pursues righteousness on his or her own, which is the grievous sin of self-righteousness.

As long as Christians fail to repent of self-righteousness, we will continue to speak of evangelism in terms such as *outreach,* which implies we will not embrace lost people but will keep them at least an arm's length away. Unrepentant self-righteousness also permits us to justify our sin by viewing ourselves as "clean" and others as "dirty," which then causes us to avoid others in an effort to remain untainted. Repentance enables us to kneel humbly with fellow sinners at the foot of the cross so they can see Jesus without our pride rising up to encumber their view.

Self-righteousness has so seeped into American Christianity that being a missionary to one's neighbors is easily overlooked because of the sickness of our faith. How sick are we when the most popular books among American Christians are about how to get blessed by praying a small section of Old Testament Scripture like a pagan mantra, and about the Rapture, as if the goal of the Christian life were to get more junk and leave this trailer park of a planet before God's tornado touches down on all the sinners? Only through repentant eyes will we see that God has a plan, by the power of the gospel of grace, to build a community of transformed people.

⊃ REDEEMING:
TRINITARIAN COMMUNITY

This new community of transformed people, called the church, should be patterned after the one true God, who eternally exists as a Trinitarian community of Father, Son, and Spirit. God made men and women in his image and likeness, which means, in part, that we too were made for friendships and community. It explains why God told our father Adam that it was not good for him to be alone, though at that time both he and his environment were perfect. God made Eve to be in friendship, marriage covenant, and community together with Adam. But they were soon separated by their sin, which came between them. Since our first parents, we have all been born into a world in which we long for gracious, joyous, and endless friendship and community but find this longing unsatisfied because of the sin that separates us from friendship with God and one another.

In his book *Bowling Alone*, Harvard professor Robert Putnam explains this phenomenon by showing that our world is arranged by various sorts of capital.[5] *Physical capital* includes the objects that we possess and use. *Human capital* includes the skills, talents, and abilities that God has given people. *Social capital* includes the friends, acquaintances, coworkers, family members, and other relationships that form a web of trust and reciprocity.

Traditionally, people have lived their lives in these social-capital networks by formally and informally bartering goods, services, information, favors, and the like. Basically, this means that I do something nice to help you because we have some type of relationship, with the understanding that, later on, you will help me when I need it, because I've made a deposit into our invisible social-capital account.

Traditionally, the largest repository of social capital has been the church.[6] Roughly half of all membership in organizations, charitable giving, and community service is connected to religious organizations, making them the number-one repository of social friendships and connecting opportunities in our nation.[7] But as spirituality has become more of a private affair, the percentage of the population that attends Protestant churches has declined from 15 percent to 12 percent in just the last quarter-century.[8] Correspondingly, in the past twenty-five years, there has been a decline in both the number of friendships and the number of organizations that people typically join to build friendships — everything from labor unions to professional associations and civic groups.[9] In addition, between 1970 and 1999, the divorce rate has tripled, the teen suicide rate has tripled, and depression has become more prevalent, which has contributed to a disconnected culture of loneliness.[10]

The decline in our nation's social capital inevitably reduces all of life to a transaction-based culture in which the only way you can get anyone to help you is to pay them. So if you are lonely and want someone to speak to, you may have to pay a counselor. If you can't pick up your dry cleaning, you may have to hire a personal assistant. If you want to work out with someone, you may have to hire a personal trainer. And if your car breaks down, you may have to call a cab — rather than a neighbor — to pick you up.

Many people are lonely and lack the community gathering points in which they can make meaningful human contacts.

The following statistics demonstrate this altering of our relational landscape in the past twenty-five years.

- Playing cards as a social activity is down 25 percent.[11]
- Frequenting bars, nightclubs, and taverns is down 40 percent.[12]
- The number of full-service restaurants has decreased 25 percent, and the number of bars (including coffee bars) and luncheonettes has decreased 50 percent, but the number of fast-food outlets has increased 100 percent, as more people eat alone and eat more meals in their cars.[13]
- Having a social evening with someone from one's neighborhood is down 33 percent.[14]
- Attending social clubs and meetings is down 58 percent.[15]
- Family dinners are down 33 percent.[16]
- Having friends over to one's home is down 45 percent.[17]
- From 1980 to 1993, participation in America's number-one participant sport, bowling, was up 10 percent, but the number of bowling leagues decreased 40 percent, as more people bowled alone.[18]
- From 1985 to 1999, the readiness of the average American to make new friends declined by nearly 33 percent.[19]

People are increasingly busy, isolated, lonely, disconnected, and without any helpful solutions in the culture. The isolation is now so entrenched that many people don't know how to practice hospitality. This trend is even reflected in new architecture, which replaces large dining and living rooms designed for human contact with walk-in closets, home offices, and personal entertainment rooms. Here lonely people can watch sitcoms about friendships and reality-based shows in which characters pretend to interact with human beings, a thing apparently fascinating and foreign to many lonely, isolated individuals.

Living alone, driving alone, eating alone, sleeping alone, having sex alone, and working alone make many people so depressed that they cope with the assistance of medication rather than human contact. Some, however, seek out human connection through groups, as 40 percent of all Americans are now in some form of group (Sunday schools, support groups, writing groups, self-improvement groups, cause-oriented groups, therapy groups, civic-betterment groups, recovery groups, weight-loss groups, literary groups), because they are dying of loneliness, particularly if they are single, and even more so if they are divorced.[20]

The time, money, and energy spent by previous generations on building friendships and community are increasingly being spent in impersonal pursuits such as pet care and beauty regimens.

- From 1992 to 1999, the amount of time spent caring for a pet increased 15 percent.[21]
- From 1992 to 1999, the amount of time spent for personal grooming increased 5–7 percent.[22]

Isn't it odd that we are apparently becoming a nation of attractive people who sit at home alone at night with our pets, watching television shows about relationships and taking medication for the depression brought on by our loneliness? Meanwhile, our neighbors, whom we do not know, are spending their evenings in much the same way.

Reformission requires that in our increasingly individualistic, lonely, and depressed culture, we avoid proclaiming solely a personal relationship with Jesus. The gospel requires us to proclaim and embody the full work of Jesus' death and resurrection. Jesus has accomplished four things which people long for. First, Jesus takes away the sins that separate us from God so that we can be connected to God, which fills our spiritual longings. Second, Jesus takes away the sins that separate us from each other so that we can be reconciled to each other as the church, which fills our social longings. Third, Jesus forgives the sins we have committed, thereby cleansing us of our filth, which fills our emotional longing for forgiveness. Fourth, Jesus cleanses us of the defilement that has come upon us through the sins of others, which fulfills our psychological longing for healing, cleansing, and new life.

In conclusion, reformission evangelism is about seeing the many real needs of people in the culture and realizing that our kindest gift is to connect them to Jesus and his people. To do so, we must delve into the culture to understand the real needs of people, which is the next issue we will examine.

➲ REFLECTING:
REFORMISSION QUESTIONS

1. What do you think are your most cumbersome sins for which Jesus died to make you a Christian?
2. Which sins has Jesus taken away so that you could be reconciled to your Christian friends?
3. Which most troubling sins has Jesus forgiven you of so that you would not have to live in guilt?
4. Which sins committed against you have defiled you most, and how has Jesus cleansed you from their stains?
5. Which people have sinned most grievously against you, and how has Jesus enabled you to forgive them?
6. In what ways are you self-righteous?
7. Name a few non-Christian family members or friends whom you are in relationship with and answer the following questions with them in mind.
    a. Which most obvious sins will they need to repent of to become Christians?
    b. How are their sins separating them from God and other people?

c. How has their sin caused them to feel guilty?

d. How have sins which have been committed against them defiled them in such a way that their identities are largely tied to those sad circumstances?

e. What unforgiving bitterness do they hold against people who have sinned against them, and how is that bitterness damaging their lives?

f. How would you best communicate the gospel to them in terms that they can relate to?

REFORMISSION INTERVIEW WITH STEF HJERTAGER
From Dancer to Deacon

1. **What is your name?**
   Stef Hjertager

2. **Do you consider yourself to be a Christian?**
   Yes

3. **What is your age?**
   26

4. **What was your vocation prior to your conversion?**
   Exotic dancer

5. **What is your current vocation and ministry?**
   Office administrator for a game development company. I am currently a serving lead and deacon for our church.

6. **Explain your conversion and how friends were vital to your salvation.**
   I was thirteen when I decided that my life needed a little change. I started smoking and drinking, and by the time I was fifteen or sixteen, I was doing and dealing drugs. I also started to have sexual relationships about that time. I spent a few years like that, then I thought life could only get better if I lived on my own. So I graduated from high school and moved out at seventeen. It was a great place. There was a needle-exchanging program at the manager's office, and there were cockroaches in the bedroom. It wasn't even an apartment; it was a motel that I paid for by the week. I couldn't afford it for long, so I decided I needed to make some quick money. After waitressing at an exotic club for a few

weeks, I realized the best money was in dancing, so I became an exotic dancer.

At the club that I was working at, I met my future husband. We became best friends right away. He convinced me that I really shouldn't be doing drugs. After a terrible overdose experience and his convincing words, I quit. About three months after we met, we moved into an apart-

ment together and decided to be an exclusive couple. A few more years went by before things started to change in our lives. God decided that it was time for me to stop running from him.

When God started to grab ahold of my life, it was a process, not a sudden moment. Greg had recently become a Christian and was holding a Bible study in our home. I was not yet interested in God at all. Greg had purchased his own Bible and was reading it at work every day. He would come home and talk about it all the time. I was raised in a very legalistic church and was kicked out when I was a teenager. From then on, I wanted nothing to do with the church or God or anything. One morning when Greg got home from work, I sat him down and told him how things were going to be. I explained to him that I didn't care if he had a Bible study in the house, I didn't care if he read the Bible or even talked about it. I just wanted nothing to do with his God or the Bible or anything. He did his thing and I did mine.

Since the study was in our home and I was playing hostess, I started to overhear the Word of God. In the beginning, I kept my distance, but over time, it really started to get to me. I was very much on a search for truth and what the Bible really did say once I started to hear more. There were things I was never taught, and I wondered if there was more that I missed.

Learning the truth was very difficult, though. At the time, it seemed that I couldn't get anything right. God was using my friends to tell me about him. To show me where in my life I wasn't living according to God's will. To be honest, I did not like their honesty. I did not like hearing that my life and the choices that I was making were not what God wanted. I didn't like hearing my friends tell me I was wrong. I didn't want to change my ways. I was sinning in my heart by fighting the advice that my friends were giving me. I was even starting to dislike my friends. I came from a place where you did what you wanted, and I did what I wanted and no one had the right to tell anyone what they were doing was wrong. However, I started to notice that God was the one who could say what I was doing was wrong. I didn't like that either.

But over time, God was gracious and started to teach my heart and mind to want his will for my life and not my own. Even though I didn't like what my friends were saying, they still kept saying it. They didn't stop telling me about God and what he wanted. For a long time, it was hard because I understood what they were saying, but I couldn't seem to do it. I really wanted to do what God wanted for my life, but I just couldn't seem to stop sinning. You know what? I learned that we won't ever stop sinning. We are that way from the core. So what

do you do? You rely on God, and only then can you do what is in his will. It is only when you are in relationship with God and trusting him that you even understand what he wishes for your life and how to then follow him without trial.

In the process of reading and studying the Bible, I started to believe. We went to a church called Mars Hill Church for a weekly Wednesday night Bible study on the book of Revelation. I was amazed at and in utter awe of how brutally honestly the pastor spoke. It was truly God speaking directly into my heart and life.

Over that summer, Greg and I spent many hours with people from the church. We had dinners and did BBQs. We just simply got to know people. But with that, we received good godly teaching from the elders and members alike. Basically, God was not thrilled with where we were in our lives, and he was taking the opportunity to let us know in a very upfront and honest way.

I was informed that my job was sinful. Mind you, I had a feeling it wasn't the best of occupations, but I was positive that God could work through that somehow and I would be able to keep dancing. In the end, it was hard to take. I didn't know how we were going to survive with so much less money per month if I quit like God asked. What I didn't understand at the time is that God is my Father. He is there to take care of me and help me when times are both good and bad. To be quite honest, my head was still spinning from really starting to understand God and what he was all about. Then to go and have to completely change my occupation was a bit of a shocker.

God also informed me that both Greg and I were living in sin. We had been living together for two and a half years at this point and knew that "someday" we would get married, but we didn't know when. We spoke to the pastor, and he let us know of our sinful situation, and we both felt compelled to get married ASAP.

So three days before we got married, Greg told me I had to quit dancing. Understand that he was still in his spiritual infancy also at this point and that laying down the law for his future wife was not an easy task. So then, after a long conversation, the decision was made, and I quit dancing. Three weeks after we had spoken to the Mars Hill pastor, we got married.

I am not exactly sure when I officially became a Christian. What I do know is that Jesus Christ died on the cross for the sins of his people. He shed more than just tears for their salvation. He suffered brutally and more than any of us will ever know. Then three days later, he rose again to conquer sin and death so that we too may rise again and live with him someday. I thank the Lord Jesus Christ for the sacrifice he made for us so that we might live again with him forever.

LOVING YOUR NEIGHBOR IN THE CULTURE

Chapter Four

ELVIS IN EDEN

A Reformission Understanding of Culture

I am so hairy that I think I'm part Wookie. Subsequently, I spend an inordinate percentage of my life shaving and sitting in a barber's chair for a haircut. Every time I get my hair cut, I undergo a cross-cultural experience. My barbershop is down the street from our church in an area known as the eccentric hangout for self-identified urban hipsters. Its claim to fame is an annual summer-solstice parade that features a nudist bicycling team. The barbershop is part of a small chain that promotes arty concerts and provides the finest selection of waiting-area pornography in our city.

On one occasion, my young son Zac and I were getting our hair cut by a large flamboyant woman with bleached-blond hair, a black concert tank top, bright red lipstick, jeans, and tattoos large enough to double as billboards. During the haircut, she fired a succession of questions at me about parenting that made me feel like a contestant on a game show. Near the end of the haircut, she thanked me for my insight, told my son that he had a good daddy, and then informed us that she was going to be a good "daddy" too.

Looking as if he had just taken a swig from a milk jug that was years past the expiration date, my son stared at me, wanting an explanation for how this woman could be a daddy. So I asked the woman if she was planning on getting pregnant. She said that she was not but that her girlfriend planned to conceive through a threesome with a male friend who liked to have sex with her and her "wife."

The woman could not have been nicer, yet she saw no difference between her marriage and mine, or my family and the one she was creating. Although we live in the same zip code, listen to the same music, and are roughly the same age, we live in very different cultures.

⊃ REMEMBERING:
CREATION AND CURSE

As Christians on reformission living in an era of pluralism, we will encounter a variety of cultures each day. Consequently, it is vital for us to understand culture as an enormous framework within which people live their lives.

Listen to a few descriptions of culture:

Cultural commentator Rodney Clapp says that culture "takes in media, advertising, information technology, fashion, ritual, worship, academic disciplines, public symbols, lifestyles and everyday practices such as automobile commuting or childbearing."[1]

Author Renato Rosaldo says, "Culture lends significance to human experience by selecting from and organizing it. It refers broadly to the forms through which people make sense of their lives, rather than more narrowly to the opera or art museums. It does not inhabit a set-aside domain.... From the pirouettes of classical ballet to the most brute of brute facts, all of human conduct is culturally mediated. Culture encompasses the everyday and the esoteric, the mundane and the elevated, the ridiculous and the sublime."[2]

Missionary pioneer Lesslie Newbigin says that "by the word culture we have to understand the sum total ways of living developed by a group of human beings and handed on from generation to generation. Central to culture is language. The language of a people provides the means by which they express their way of perceiving things and of coping with them. Around that center one would have to group their visual and musical arts, their technologies, their law, and their social and political organization. And one must also include in culture, and as fundamental to any culture, a set of beliefs, experiences, and practices that seek to grasp and express the ultimate nature of things, that which gives shape and meaning to life, that which claims final loyalty. I am speaking, obviously, about religion. Religion — including the Christian religion — is thus part of culture."[3]

People live in culture as naturally as fish live in water and tornados hit trailer parks. But most people are as unaware of their cultural assumptions as they are of their bad breath, because it is so familiar to them. Therefore, Christians on reformission must be particularly attentive to both the culture they live in and the other cultures they encounter.

While arguably every academic discipline depends on understanding the *what* of culture, only Christian theology can explain the *why* of culture. People create culture because God made them to fill, work, and keep the earth.

But because of sin, the innate desire God has placed within us to create culture has become bent and crooked. In Genesis, fallen culture begins with a welcoming of Satan, evil, chaos, lies, Scripture-twisting, a weak man's abdication of leadership, coveting, shame, separation between people, running from God, blaming others for sin, family strife, and death. The fulfillment of this cursed culture will be the eternal torments of hell.

Cultures are hard to untangle and understand because they reflect both the beauty of creation and the ugliness of the Fall. To help us better untangle the various cultures that we encounter, allow me to share some perspectives. For the purposes of this book, it will be beneficial for you to think in terms of the people who live near you, because that is where your reformission evangelism occurs. Remember that every culture can mediate the gospel if we expend the effort to determine how to work through that culture. Our ultimate goal is to have people from every culture worshiping Jesus through their culture — the vision gloriously pictured in the book of Revelation.

HOW TO EVALUATE CULTURE: THOUGHTS, VALUES, AND EXPERIENCES

One way to study a culture and what motivates people to order their lives in particular ways is to examine what they do. Much of what the people in a culture do is determined by how they think, what they value, and what experiences have shaped them as a people. These are the essential ingredients of a culture, which explains why many people gather in tribes around them.

Thought tribes. The first ingredient of a culture is the cognitive aspect, or how its people think and arrive at their beliefs. For example, are the people who live within a few miles of you more likely to make decisions by academic rigor or emotional hunch, family consensus or individual perspective, consistency with tradition or desire for innovation, personal interest or community benefit, or some other way of thinking? In academic ivory towers, this branch of philosophy falls under the category of epistemology. On the street, it is simply the answer to the perennial question, "Whaddya do that fer?"

While it is important to recognize that ideas have consequences, I would discourage overemphasizing the cognitive aspect of your culture. It is common — particularly as the windfalls and pitfalls of postmodernism are debated in the fools' parade of books on the matter — for Christians to believe there is a cause-and-effect relationship between the actions and philosophical framework underlying any person's moral decision-making process.

The truth is that most people are contradictions, neither logical nor coherent in their reasoning. Like the guy who put the following bumper stickers on his truck: "Meat Is Murder" along with "Keep Abortion Safe and Legal," and "Jesus Is My Copilot" along with "The Goddess Is Alive and Magic Is Afoot." And who hasn't stood in line at a coffee shop behind someone ordering scones the size of North and South Carolina along with a bucket of coffee bathed in chocolate — with, of course, low-fat milk to keep them from gaining weight?

Most people don't spend time discussing the differences between early and late Wittgenstein and the effects of his thought on their moral decision-making because they are preoccupied with whether their jeans make their butts look big or if it's just that their big butts make their butts look big.

Values tribes. The second ingredient of a culture are the values that are often so widely assumed that they are rarely articulated or defended. Behind the ordering of lives and cultures, these values compel the decisions and sacrifices people make in devoting themselves to possessions, status, experiences, causes, and movements.

For example, in my city of Seattle, people value independence, which explains why they are likely to be single, to cohabitate, and to avoid having children. Commitments such as marriage and parenting would require them to live sacrificially, undermining their independence. Their value of independence also explains why Seattleites tend to prefer independent bookstores, coffee shops, music stores, record labels, rock bands, restaurants, and clothing stores over national chains and products. It also explains why they are reluctant to attend church and embrace a spirituality that requires that a denomination, a theology, a pastor, the Bible, or even Jesus be in authority over them.

The trick to uncovering people's values is to assess how they invest their time, energy, money, and passion. What do they love and what do they hate? What do they talk about? What do they rally around? But values can be tricky because they are often little more than ideals, what people merely wish they valued and cared for, what they are committed to in theory but not in practice. Many vegetarians eat meat, environmentalists don't recycle, employees don't work, and Christians don't read their Bibles. Ideals are what you want; values are what you do. Ideals become values only if they are lived out.

Experience tribes. The third ingredient of a culture are the experiences that shape people. Some experiences are chosen by people because they enjoy them. A quick scan of the magazine rack at your local store can reveal the passion various cultures have for sex, hobbies, home-improvement projects, drug use, film, music, sports, cigar smoking, off-road driving, cars, home theaters, and fitness.

Some experiences are forced on people. These experiences are likely to be devastating and painful, but they shape a person nonetheless. Having conducted premarital counseling for over one hundred couples during my first five years as a pastor, I am devastated by the number of people who have been sexually abused as children and the effects that sin had on their lives.

All of these ingredients (thinking, values, and experiences) combine to create the cultures in which people live. From the outside, these cultures can easily be misunderstood. For example, some people at our church dress in a gothic fashion, complete with faces painted white, hair dyed black, and dark clothing. I was speaking with a visiting pastor once before a church service when a woman dressed in this style walked by, and the pastor commented that it was good for the woman to be in church because she obviously needed to meet Jesus and overcome her depression. But the woman he spoke of was a leader in our church and a godly woman who dressed that way because of her sense of personal style. She was in no way depressed.

To be faithful in reformission, we must embed ourselves in a culture and develop friendships with lost people so that we can be informed and avoid making erroneous judgments. Non-Christian friends actually help to disciple us in culture as we evangelize them in Christ. For example, the president of the chamber of commerce in our neighborhood has become a good friend to a pastor at our church. Though he is not a Christian, he has done a tremendous amount to teach us about the history and future of our local culture and how we can best embed ourselves in it. He's even placed one of our pastors on the chamber of commerce board to help shape our local culture. Because we care about the same culture he does, he sees us as allies and friends, even though he is aware that our hope is that he and other people would come to love Jesus. Friends like this are invaluable to reformission.

In addition to understanding the cultures around your church, you also need to be aware that your church has a culture of its own. Reformission requires that we ask the same hard questions about the thinking, values, and experiences that shape our church cultures. We must then evaluate our findings in the light of Scripture to measure how faithful we are being to God. This will help to ensure that we are not hypocritically judging the cultures around us while neglecting to judge our own. For instance, a very overweight pastor friend of mine continually preaches against smoking, which is not mentioned in the Bible, while he conveniently ignores the buffet of verses on gluttony because the values in his church are different from those of the surrounding cultures and of the Scriptures.

Last, the thoughts, values, and experiences of a culture present both opportunities and obstacles for the gospel. The better we understand a culture, the better prepared we will be to reach that culture so that God can transform how people think, what they value, and how they experience life.

HOW TO EVALUATE CULTURE: HIGH, FOLK, AND POP

Another way we can evaluate a culture is by examining the various styles within it, including its subcultures. Christian cultural commentator Ken Myers explains that culture exists in the three forms: high, folk, and pop.[4]

High culture is like a gourmet meal prepared and served by professionals. It is marked by a connection to traditions of the past, which requires training, patience, reflection, and a cultivated ability to enjoy and appreciate. High culture is commonly referred to as art. Examples would include opera, classical music, and ballet.

Folk culture is like a home-cooked meal made from scratch using a family recipe. It emerges from a particular community of people as an expression and extension of their lives together, and it is highly enduring because it is part of who they are. Because of its community aspect, folk culture flourishes in rural areas, smaller towns, and in the neighborhoods of larger cities, which function to some degree as enclaves or tribes with particular values and styles that bind people together. These variables make folk culture highly personal, endearing, and enduring. Examples of folk culture would include black spiritual songs that have endured for generations as the articulation of the life of a community, and some forms of independent punk rock.

Pop culture is like a fast-food meal ordered from a drive-up window and cooked by a high-school kid in a uniform who wants to know if you would prefer to supersize your order. It is intended for mass audiences and lacks the sophistication of high culture and the personal touch of folk culture. Pop culture has spread with the growth of American cities and suburbs. While pop culture is more accessible, it also requires less engagement and is more fleeting, trite, disposable, and faddish. It values the individual over the community, newness over tradition, and instant experience over patience. Pop culture also features someone's personality over the quality of their work and is becoming more difficult to distinguish from advertising. Examples of pop culture are legion, because since the 1960s it has been the dominant American culture. It is perhaps best exemplified by Michael Jackson, who in an effort to not fade from pop cultural popularity, continually reinvented his image so thoroughly that he transformed from a black man to a white woman.

While each of these cultural forms can mediate the gospel (arguably some more easily than others), this fact is often overlooked because people tend to attach a moral value to the cultural form they prefer. This is also true in the church, as can be seen in the "worship wars," clashes between people who prefer different styles of worship music and perceive their preferred cultural form as more devout than others. Isn't this simply a debate as to whether God should be worshiped through high, folk, or pop cultural forms?

For example, in some churches, people desire to sing old hymns led by an organ and a robed choir (high culture). But their desire conflicts with people who want to sing contemporary praise songs led by a band wearing casual clothes and playing keyboards and acoustic guitars (pop culture). But their desire conflicts with people who want to burn the hymnal and ignore contemporary Christian worship music, to write their own songs and perform them with amplifiers cranked so loud that they blow a wind strong enough to part the Red Sea (folk culture). Some churches caught in the crossfire have resorted to a blended form of worship in which all three styles are used in the same service, which is often about as tasty as having a vintage merlot with your Big Mac.

Why is this significant? Because issues of style and culture affect how you live your life, how you worship God, and how you will be perceived by lost people in your culture. In practical terms, your cultural preferences help determine the way you dress, where you live, what you drive, the entertainment you enjoy, whom you trust, what friends you have, and how you perceive and communicate the gospel.

Do you spot the cultural issue for reformission churches? Our challenge is to determine whether the cultural form that dominates how we do life when gathered for worship and scattered for mission is best suited for evangelizing the people in our community. This is a crucial matter because even declining churches are often unable to see that the cultural form through which they mediate the gospel each week is failing to reach people. Some churches and leaders do not see their failure because the few Christians who attend their church do so because they enjoy it, find it meaningful, and therefore do not consider that they are a declining cultural minority.

Reformission Christians and churches exist to perpetuate the gospel and should be swift to change their cultural forms if they are not the most beneficial for achieving that goal. This is what Paul told the Corinthians about being all things to all people and using all means to see as many people as possible saved (1 Cor. 9:19–23). Reformission churches have to continually examine and adjust their musical styles, websites, aesthetics, acoustics, programming, and just about everything but their Bible in an effort to effectively communicate the gospel to as many people as possible in the cultures around them.

HOW TO EVALUATE CULTURE: WAVES

Another way to untangle culture is by understanding what futurist Alvin Toeffler describes as three chronological waves of change that have crashed upon the beach of the Western world.[5] The first wave was an *agricultural age*, in which people were primarily concerned with survival through working the land with their hands. The agricultural age peaked in the United States in the eighteenth century, when more than 80 percent of the workforce was employed on farms.[6] Today, less than 3 percent of Americans work on farms.[7]

The second wave was an *industrial age,* in which people were primarily concerned with efficiency and building machines and industrial centers to increase automation and production. By the 1880s, the United States had overtaken England as the world's leading manufacturer. Subsequently, many Americans moved from their farms to the city to work in factories. But today, manufacturing jobs employ only 17 percent of the U.S. population.[8]

The third wave is our current *technological age,* in which people are primarily concerned with exchanging information and experiences. The technological age arguably began with the invention of the telephone and leaped forward with the creation of the internet. While it took the telephone seventy years to penetrate the homes of 75 percent of the American population,[9] it took the internet just seven years to achieve the same result. Amazingly, the presence of DVD players leaped from 18 percent to 56 percent in just three years, and the technological age continues to flourish.[10]

In our technological age, Christian institutions such as denominations, missions organizations, and theological institutions that had their beginning in the agricultural and industrial ages are finding it increasingly difficult to thrive. This is in part because the values driving our national culture have transitioned from the big eating the small, to the fast eating the slow. In previous cultural waves, centralizing power, standardizing systems, and creating large organizations were the keys to longevity and respect. But many of these churches and organizations were slow to react to cultural changes because their size made responding difficult. In our present cultural wave, the keys to survival are the decentralizing of power, the flexibility of systems, and the creation of smaller independent organizations that can band together as needed for particular tasks. In practice, Christians and churches on reformission first need to assess which cultural wave they are in now and which cultural wave they will be in during the next five years. Then with this knowledge in hand, they need to reorganize themselves so they'll be able to quickly respond to the changing demands of the cultures around them.

HOW TO EVALUATE CULTURE: SINS AND SINS

Another way to evaluate culture is by examining the universal and particular sins common in that culture. *Universal sins* are those offenses which the Bible condemns for all people in all cultures, including sexual immorality, idolatry, adultery, prostitution, homosexuality, theft, drunkenness, greed, slander, and swindling (1 Cor. 6:9–10) — or the central elements of most television shows.

Particular sins are those offenses that are sinful for some people under some circumstances but not for all people under all circumstances. All Christians are commanded by God to avoid universal sins. But Christians are also commanded by God to avoid sins that are particular to them, without unfairly condemning or restricting the freedoms of fellow Christians who involve themselves differently in controversial cultural matters. For example, I personally disdain cigarettes, but I cannot forbid everyone in my church from smoking, because the Bible does not. This is, in part, what Paul means throughout the New Testament when he speaks of weak and strong Christians. In truth, every Christian is both weak and strong. So in some areas, we all need to restrict our freedoms because of our weaknesses, while we are able to use our Christian liberty in areas in which we are strong.

Reformission recognizes that Christians will have differing personal convictions in matters of culture and welcomes those differences that are not sinful, because what pleases God is unity, not uniformity. Uniformity undermines reformission and often is promoted by erroneous restrictive and permissive theologies. Restrictive Christians go too far and name everything a universal sin, forbidding some cultural activities that the Bible does not, such as listening to certain musical styles, getting tattoos, watching movies, smoking cigarettes, consuming alcohol, and body piercing. Conversely, permissive churches are prone to naming everything a particular sin and bless activities which the Bible forbids, such as drug use, fornication, homosexuality, and cohabitation before marriage.

I'm not advocating either a permissive or a restrictive approach to debatable cultural issues. Rather, I am encouraging Christians on reformission to involve themselves in their local cultures not merely for the purpose of entertainment but primarily for the purpose of education. As a missionary, you will need to watch television shows and movies, listen to music, read books, peruse magazines, attend events, join organizations, surf websites, and befriend people that you might not like to better understand people that Jesus loves. I often read magazines intended for teenage girls, not because I need to take tests to discover if I am compatible with my boyfriend or because I need leg-waxing tips, but because I want to see young women meet Jesus, and so I want to understand them better.

Last, reformission understands that Scripture is replete with principles that give us wisdom in our decision-making. So as you consider an area of your culture that you are unsure about participating in, these principles will help you determine if that activity would be a particular sin for you. The importance of this matter became clear to me after witnessing the experience of a Christian friend. She is a gifted designer who ran a specialty wedding-invitation business. One of her prospective clients was a homosexual couple seeking to have a same-sex union, and she was torn over whether she should obey the city ordinance that recognized such relationships, or her conscience, which did not permit her to participate. After prayerfully wrestling with the issue, she turned away the prospective clients, and when they asked if it was because they were gay, she told the truth and said that though she had no ill will toward them, she was not comfortable with being involved. She soon found herself maligned in the media by various gay-rights advocates, and the opposition eventually forced her to shut down her business. As our culture becomes increasingly less tolerant of Christian principles, it is important that God's people operate with discernment, and I hope that the following principles will help guide your cultural decision-making.

⮑ REPENTING:
LIKE JONAH DID

Once we have searched our conscience and the Scriptures to determine in what ways we can participate in our culture, we must then obey the Bible's command to love our neighbor. Note that the Bible does not call us to *like* our neighbor. The reason

---

Biblical Principles for Cultural Decision-Making

- Is it beneficial to me personally and to the gospel generally (1 Cor. 6:12)?
- Will I lose self-control and be mastered by what I participate in (1 Cor. 6:12)?
- Will I be doing this in the presence of someone who I know will fall into sin as a result (1 Cor. 8:9–10)?
- Is it a violation of the laws of my city, state, or nation (Rom. 13:1–7)?
- If I fail to do this, will I lose opportunities to share the gospel (1 Cor. 10:27–30)?
- Can I do this with a clear conscience (Acts 24:16)?
- Will this cause me to sin by feeding sinful desires (Rom. 13:13–14)?
- Am I convinced that this is what God desires for me to do (Rom. 13:5)?
- Does my participation proceed from my faith in Jesus Christ (Rom. 14:23)?
- Am I doing this to help other people, or am I just being selfish (1 Cor. 10:24)?
- Can I do this in a way that glorifies God (1 Cor. 10:31–33)?
- Am I following the example of Jesus Christ to help save sinners (1 Cor. 10:33–11:1)?

for this distinction is because every culture is filled with people who are about as pleasant to be around as receiving a blow from a roofing hammer to your frontal lobe. Some Christians refuse to be about reformission simply because they avoid people they find unpleasant.

The book of Jonah is particularly helpful in shedding some light on this tendency. During the time of Jonah, the nation of Israel was much like our own nation — financially prosperous but spiritually impoverished. The bitter enemy of Israel was Assyria, whose resume included witchcraft, murder, prostitution, drunkenness, cruelty, and pride (Nahum 3). One of the principal Assyrian cities was Nineveh, which was fortified by hundred-foot walls surrounding the city. The walls were wide enough for three chariots to run atop side by side, and made these sinners feel invincible.

God commanded Jonah to go east to preach to Nineveh, but instead Jonah fled south to Tarshish. Before long, he was swallowed by an enormous fish that likely smelled like an outhouse at a county fair. Usually, when a man eats bad fish, he vomits, but in this case, the fish ate a bad man and vomited him up, near Nineveh of course.

Realizing that he would not win his fight with God, Jonah entered Nineveh and simply said, "Forty more days and Nineveh will be overturned." Those words exploded through the great city, dropping half a million people to their knees in brokenness, repentance, and fear of the Lord.

In the concluding chapter of the book, Jonah's heart is exposed, and the reasons for his running are revealed in his frank and irreverent argument with God. Following the greatest revival in the history of the world, Jonah was happy to receive God's grace but furious to see it extended to people he did not like.

God, who got the first word in the book, also got the last word. He rebuked Jonah for loving a plant that shaded his head more than he loved the Ninevites. And the book brings us all, like Jonah, under the conviction that we love the things God has given us — homes, cars, hobbies, health, friends — more than our great cities and the spiritually blind people who annoy us. We pass these people every day and ignore them because our minds are consumed with ourselves rather than with our God and our neighbor.

Throughout the book, Jonah simply looks wicked — at least as wicked as the pagans he was sent to preach to. But I believe that God continued to pursue Jonah long after the events concluded in Nineveh and that eventually the prophet was brought to repentance. This would explain why the book was written. If Jonah had remained unrepentant, we would expect the book to vindicate him as the victim of a mean God who nearly drowned him, later gave him third-degree burns, and spanked his inner child. Or we would expect the book to simply record the greatest revival in history, with Jonah taking all the credit for being such a phenomenal preacher. Or perhaps the book never would have been written at all. But instead, we get an honest glimpse of exactly how sinful Jonah was, how gracious God is, and what kind of self-righteous, racist prig Jonah would be without God.

To this day, the Jews gather in the synagogue each year on the Day of Atonement to read Jonah. After the reading, they reply, "We are Jonah." This truth is essential for rightly relating to Jonah. We are Jonah when, because we do not like them, we run from God's call on our lives to bring the gospel to lost people, whom he loves. We are Jonah because we too have been sent to proclaim repentance to great but wicked cities filled with people like the Ninevites — people whom God loves but we don't like.

And Jonah leaves us to ponder who we would be if God had stopped running after us and simply left us to ourselves. In what ways are we running from God's call to bring the gospel to others? What will repentance look like for us? What could happen if God captured the hearts of people in your town because you pointed them to him? What if the heart God's people had for their cities was like Jesus' heart for Jerusalem instead of like Jonah's heart for Nineveh?

➲ REDEEMING:
THE HEART OF CULTURE

Jesus wept over the condition of Jerusalem. Once we have repented of our sin of indifference, we too will weep over our towns and long for their transformation. The question persists, How can such change occur?

For the past two hundred years, the answer has been debated in a bitter fight between two ideologies. In his book *A Conflict of Visions: Ideological Origins of Political Struggles,* social commentator Thomas Sowell deftly explains that the political conflict between the right (Republican) and the left (Democrat) stems from vastly differing understandings of human nature.[11]

Sowell defines the two visions for the transformation of our culture as "constrained" and "unconstrained." The constrained (Republican) vision views human nature as selfishly sinful and places its hope in restraining our sin through the law. The unconstrained (Democratic) vision is diametrically opposed to this. It optimistically perceives human nature as basically good and capable of perfection in this life through social planning, including public education, government programs, and social services. The one thing the two visions have in common is that their faith rests in institutions; they simply disagree as to whether these institutions should release us or restrain us.

But our faith rests in Jesus alone, who redeems people and their cultures. Reformission requires that we get off these tired tracks on which Republican and Democratic politics run. Instead, we should focus our attention on the gospel because our ultimate hope rests in God, not in human governments, programs, or institutions.

To understand both the human problem and the divine solution, we must begin at the beginning. After his sin, our first father, Adam, blamed his dissatisfaction with his culture on his wife and the God who made her. We, his children, follow in Adam's footsteps when we blame our dissatisfaction with life on something or someone "out there" in the culture (our parents, school, church, nation), rather than on something within us (pride, folly, sin, selfishness, rebellion). This pattern of blame remains popular because people are more inclined to see themselves as victims than as sinners.

St. Paul calls sin the mystery of iniquity, and human history has proven him right. The problem with every culture is not ultimately "out there" in the culture but is within the people of the culture. This mystery of the crookedness of human nature has puzzled lost people in the culture so fully that we now have a veritable army of counselors and psychologists armed with some two hundred different therapeutic systems trying to straighten people out. These systems speculate that the causes of our imperfection range from an unconscious mind filled with primal urges (Sigmund Freud), to a collective unconsciousness from our racial history (Carl Jung), to our environmental (emotional and physical) conditioning (B. F. Skinner), to the lack of awareness of our inner goodness (Carl Rogers). All we are missing is a theory in which a magic bunny — hidden deep in the drink cooler of a Provo, Utah, convenience store — is the center of an invisible web of mind control causing human beings to do terrible things to one another. Reformission requires that God's people address sin theologically.

First, to change a culture, we must change the people in that culture. The question that arises is whether people do what they are, or if they are what they do. The answer to this is imperative, because if we are what we do, then all we need to do is train people to act differently, and they will change themselves. But if we do what we are, then we do bad because we are bad, and we cannot do good until we become good, the very thing which bad people cannot do, no matter how many dollars are spent and organizations are founded to help them.

The Bible clearly teaches that we do what we are. It also repeatedly teaches (particularly in Proverbs and in the teachings of Jesus) that our sin comes from our hearts, the center of who we are. Our heart is a rock band, and culture is a loudspeaker, and if we don't like the music, spending lots of money to fund organizations to "fix" the speakers won't change the tune. To rightly diagnose any human conduct, we must overcome our propensity to deal merely with cultural effects (lying, adultery, theft) and instead focus on the cause (the sin in our hearts). The sinful nature of our hearts is the root of all cultural problems and sins. The unredeemed heart is a glutton for sin and death. Only God can give a person a new heart, one with new desires for a redeemed life that contributes to a transformed culture.

Second, if we aspire to straighten out crooked people, we must define what a "good person" is. This too has been the source of much conflict because there is little agreement as to what constitutes this good person we aspire to become. The Bible teaches that Jesus of Nazareth, who lived on the earth some two thousand years ago, was God in human flesh. And though Jesus was tempted as we are, he remained without sin. Because of this, he was the perfect person and is our perfect example of what a person is supposed to be. People must compare themselves with Jesus to see their sin. Only by seeing Jesus can anyone be aware of the sin they need to repent of so that Jesus can redeem them to be like him.

In conclusion, if we aspire to seek any change in our culture, we must resist the temptation to first change the culture. Instead, we must begin by bringing the gospel to people so that they can be given a new heart out of which a Christian life flows. As more people live out of their new heart, new families, churches, businesses, and governments will result that together will transform culture.

➲ REFLECTING:
REFORMISSION QUESTIONS

1. What are the dominant thoughts, values, and life experiences that have shaped you and your church? What are the similarities and differences between your thoughts, values, and experiences and those of the average lost person in your culture?

2. Do you prefer high, folk, or pop culture? Does your church mediate the gospel primarily through high, folk, or pop culture? Where do high, folk, and pop cultures exist in your local culture?

3. What are the agricultural, industrial, and technological aspects of your culture? Which is dominant? Which are you most connected to? Which are the people in your church most connected to?

4. For what issues in your culture do you need wisdom and discernment to understand? In what areas are you culturally weak? In what areas are you culturally strong? For you, what sins are particular sins, instead of universal sins?

5. Do you have a new heart that loves God, hates sin, and causes you to become a new person more like Jesus? If so, in what ways has your new heart caused change in your life?

6. In what ways have you or your church wrongly sought to change people's behavior (including your own) rather than first focusing on their hearts?

7. In what ways have you or your church placed faith in institutions to change people at the expense of placing your faith in God and in God's working through you?

REFORMISSION INTERVIEW WITH CRASH

What Would Jesus Tattoo?

1. What is your name?

Crash

2. Do you consider yourself to be a Christian?

Yes

3. What is your age?

33

4. What is your vocation?

I own several tattoo studios and a new tattoo magazine, and I write for several international tattoo publications.

5. What services does your business provide?

Tattoos and piercings

6. What is your ministry?

Revealing the truth of the gospel to everyone I come in contact with, primarily people between eighteen and thirty-five, and many who are very unlikely to set foot in a traditional church setting.

7. Why is the popularity of tattoos and piercings growing?

Nothing more than a growing and changing culture. The primary purpose is to express individuality. Much less common is the attempt to stand in defiance of conventional belief systems, but over the last ten years, this motivation has diminished drastically as society has become more and more accepting of these expressions.

8. Do you consider yourself a missionary to your culture?

I feel that I was put in this particular profession for the purpose of reaching this postmodern generation with the truth of the gospel in the arena of a desperate, lost, and angry culture. My goal every day is not to target and convert anyone but to look for opportunities when I might be able to show Christ's love to people who have never once been shown what the real message of the gospel is. What they have been told, and what they've seen themselves, are the lies of legalism maquerading as the gospel, and "quick to judge and condemn" Christians pointing their fingers at them.

9. How have Christians responded to your ministry?

Though they are few and far between, I have encountered several great men who have hearts for the lost and who have provided encouragement to me personally. It is most unfortunate that the vast majority of "Christians" that I have encountered arbitrarily dismiss this generation as "lost" or, worse, unworthy of their time and attention. There is a tendency among Christians to confuse culture with sin and thereby condemn anyone who does not conform to their own fashions, never seeing the damage they have done to the cause of Christ.

From what I see in the Gospels, Jesus preached to society from within the culture of his day, not from above it as the Pharisees did. In my opinion, the majority of churches today are more concerned with converting one cultural image into their own cultural image, with the implication that theirs is "Christian" (where no one drinks alcohol or listens to secular music and everyone dresses in business attire), while those cultures

which differ from their view are not. Once again, this is definitively pharisaical. Unfortunately, I find this sums up the majority of the church world all too well.

For us to make any real difference in this age, we need to recognize the power of the gospel to change lives, that we were called from within a particular cultural setting, and that it is our duty to try to spread the good news of the gospel from within that setting. To simply take the gospel and leave our culture, not its sin, is to steal potential from the kingdom. We are to be "in the world but not of the world"; to me this speaks of our culture and how we are to affect those around us who

might not otherwise receive the truth, all without being held captive by the sins which are within every culture. "Sheep among wolves," so to speak.

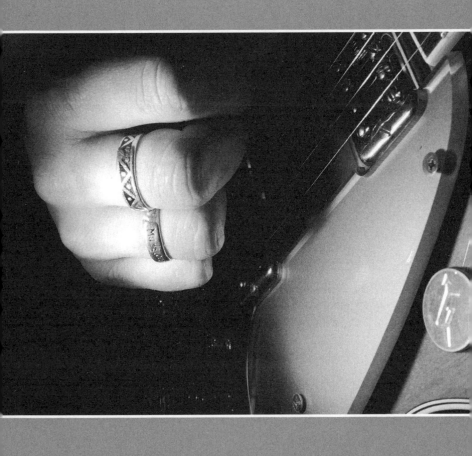

Chapter Five

GOING TO SEMINARY AT THE GROCERY STORE

Connecting with Culture in Reformission

A dear friend invited me to travel to India to speak at a conference for Indian church-planters who were doing reformission in small rural villages that had never heard of Jesus Christ. Shortly after landing at an airport in India, I found myself trying to negotiate a ride with the driver of a rickshaw, which is basically a cross between a bicycle, a motorcycle, and a cart — an effective form of both transportation and suicide. The driver of this Kevorkian Cart and I did not speak the same language, and so communication was nearly impossible. I found myself foolishly speaking slowly and loudly to him in an effort to explain where I needed to travel. But the problem wasn't that the man was deaf or stupid; he was simply from another culture.

Likewise, our nation is filled with a seemingly endless number of cultures that do not understand what the church is saying, even if they do speak the same language. In this way, our day is quite similar to the days when the gospel first spread throughout the Roman Empire, which was filled with a variety of cultures. We need to be like our New Testament brothers and sisters, seeking to bring the gospel to the cultures around us in a way that is faithful to Scripture and accessible to those cultures, be they first-generation immigrants or skateboarding teenagers and their single-parent mothers. One of the greatest mentors for us is the apostle Paul, who was chosen by God for the difficult task of bringing the gospel, which had become embedded in Jewish culture, to unreached Gentile cultures.

➲ REMEMBERING:
PAUL ON MARS HILL

As a traveling apostle, Paul's custom was to preach the gospel first to the Jews and then to the Gentiles. Because the Jews had the Old Testament Scriptures, Paul began with the Scriptures as common ground, using the Jews' prophets, theological categories, language, and teaching style to prove that Jesus was the fulfillment of all that their Scriptures had promised and for which they had eagerly waited.

But when working among Gentiles, Paul employed different methods and language to convey the same gospel. A good example is his approach on Mars Hill (Acts 17:16–34). Athens had been home to Socrates, Plato, Aristotle, and Alexander the Great, and possessed a proud heritage as one of the greatest cultural centers in the history of the world. As Paul first entered Athens, he was burdened by the great need of a people who had unparalleled philosophy, literature, architecture, art, and education but did not have Jesus. As he made the five-mile walk into town, he was troubled by the numerous idols that littered the land, and he longed for the transformation of Athens.

Paul began his ministry in Athens by proclaiming the gospel to the Jews in the synagogue. Then he continued his proclamation of the gospel in the Agora marketplace, where vendors, farmers, healers, magicians, performers, and philosophers collected in the open courtyard that served as the gathering place for the city — the easiest place to draw a crowd.

Because the Athenians had never heard about the Jesus whom Paul was preaching, they brought him before the Areopagus ("Mars Hill" in Latin), which was the Athenian court of perhaps thirty philosophers who sat as the judges of Athens, entrusted with guarding Athenian philosophy by evaluating any new ideas brought into the city. Paul stood before the court in the same place where Socrates had defended his own teachings some 450 years earlier. They asked Paul to explain his teachings, and a crowd gathered to hear the exchange. Mars Hill was that day's equivalent of television talk shows in which audience members with gaps in their teeth large enough to hold corn cobs stand up to lecture fellow mental midgets on pressing social issues with pithy counsel such as, "You need a girl with more junk in her trunk."

Courageously, Paul stood alone to proclaim the gospel, beginning by respectfully establishing common ground with his hearers so he could work from their culture to the Scriptures. His method was the reverse of his approach in the synagogue, where he worked from the Scriptures to the culture. He noted that the Athenians were a spiritual people, as was he. But he also noted that their spirituality did not include an understanding of who God is.

Like people in our own day, the Athenians were very spiritual yet in their ignorance embraced pluralism and a wide assortment of gods. A popular saying from Petronius was, "It is easier to find a god in Athens than a man." The ancient historian Pliny recorded that in the time of Nero (the 60s), Athens had over thirty thousand public statues, in addition to countless private statues in homes, all dedicated to various gods.

The circumstances leading to the creation of the altars that Paul saw littering the landscape began six hundred years before, when Athens was struck with a plague. Hundreds of people were ill and dying, and the city grew desperate to pacify the capricious gods whom they believed were tormenting them. The poet Epimenides devised a plan to appease the gods by letting sheep roam the city freely, trusting that the various gods would lead the sheep to lay down near their temple, where they could then be sacrificed to appease that moody local deity. But many sheep laid down in places where there were no temples, and so it was assumed that there must be gods that they had not known about who ruled over these areas. To pacify these gods, they erected altars to them, upon which they sacrificed the sheep. Because they did not know the name of these deities, they simply inscribed "to an unknown god" on the altars.

Paul used the opportunity provided by the culture as a starting point for the proclamation of the gospel. He began by explaining God as the creator who is separate from creation (in refutation of the Athenian's pantheism) and as the king who rules over all of heaven and earth (in refutation of their belief that gods ruled over only certain geographic regions). He continued by explaining that God does not live in temples built by men (in refutation of their belief that gods need homes like people do), and that he is utterly self-existent, not dependant on people for anything (unlike their concept of the gods as capricious humans with supernatural powers), but is in fact the sole source of all life and breath (in refutation of their pantheism). Paul then explained that God created one man and that from that one man he made all men and nations of the earth and determined exactly when and where they would live (in refutation of their Epicurean belief that life is little more than random chance) so that people would seek him and find him (in refutation of their Stoic fatalism) because he has drawn near to people (in refutation of their belief that the gods are either not distinct from people and creation or so transcendent that they cannot be known).

Picking a fight by denouncing their proud philosophical and religious history as ignorance and error where necessary, Paul also embraced the aspects of their culture that were helpful to his mission. For example, Paul quoted Epimenides, who had written of the great Greek god Zeus, "In him we live and move and have our being." Paul also quoted the Greek poet Aratus, who wrote of Zeus approximately three hundred years before, "We are his offspring." In so doing, Paul affirmed some of their spiritual concepts but showed that they were wrongly applied to Zeus and should instead be applied to Jesus. In our day, this would be akin to unearthing partial truths about God from a culture's film, music, comedy, sports, literature, theater, philosophy, economics, medicine, or politics and working from those truths to the truth of Jesus as the ultimate answer to all human questions and cultural problems.

Paul then commanded them to repent of their false notions of God, idolatry, and years of ignorant spirituality, because Jesus had risen physically from death (in refutation of both the Epicurean belief that there is no resurrection and the Stoic belief that the resurrection is not physical). Upon hearing about the resurrection, the reactions of those present on Mars Hill ranged, as they always do upon the proclamation of the gospel, from curiosity, to contempt, to conversion.

God used Paul's faithfulness to bring the gospel from Paul's Jewish culture to the Greek culture of Athens, and also to move between cultures within the Greek culture, as illustrated by both Dionysius and Damaris being given new hearts that trusted in Jesus. Dionysius was a philosopher and a member of the Mars Hill court who was likely a well-educated, powerful, and affluent man who became the pastor of the first Christian church in Athens and died a martyr's death. Damaris was likely a common woman, since no title is given for her. But because of God's grace, the Jewish Paul, the powerful and rich Greek man Dionysius, and the simple Greek woman Damaris were reconciled to God and each other through Jesus Christ.

➲ REPENTING:
BAD THEOLOGY

You and I live in our own Mars Hill, as do all of God's people. Surrounding us are multitudes of lost people who hold false notions of spirituality, God, and salvation; many of them even wrongly believe they are Christians. This point was made particularly poignant to me while taking a private tour of MTV Studios in Times Square with some friends who are fellow pastors. After meeting veejays like Matt Pinfield and passing artists like Jewel in the hallway, we were privileged to spend some time in a conference room with a young woman who was the director of marketing. She explained that MTV had likely done more demographic research on emerging generations than any other organization and found that they were very spiritual and devoted to such things as a confident belief in God and a commitment to a life of prayer. When we asked what young people thought of God, however, her answer was very Athenian. She explained that the young people they had studied believed in God and spoke to him but had no idea who he is.

While some Christians lament the condition of our spiritual but post-Christian nation, reformission sees our day as a great opportunity for the gospel, not unlike Paul's day on Mars Hill. But numerous errors in Christian theology restrain us from going to Mars Hill, seeing any idols, talking to any pagans, or quoting any godless songwriters, who are unknowingly dancing around the truth some of the time. Before we seek to be helpful to our cultural context, we must first correct any erroneous theological assumptions we may have. Here are some of the more common Christian myths about culture that may be hindering your reformission.

MYTH 1: CULTURE AND WORLDLINESS

Worldliness is the collective sinfulness that flows from human hearts to pollute God's good creation. Worldliness shows up in everything: nations, causes, movements, agendas, technologies, governments, businesses, philosophies, entertainment, and social structures of all sorts that promote the lusts of our flesh and of our wandering eyes. It exalts our pride and gives us cause to boast in ourselves rather than in God.

To help define what the Bible means by worldliness, we must mention the teachings of Jesus and his disciples. Jesus taught that Christians are no longer of this world but instead are citizens of the kingdom that is not of this world.

Echoing Jesus, the writers of the New Testament condemn worldliness. John tells us not to love this world,[1] because it is passing away,[2] it cannot understand us,[3] and it will hate us as it did our Lord,[4] while it loves liars who proclaim God's approval of this world in its present state of war against him.[5]

James tells us that part of our religious duty is to keep ourselves from being polluted by this world,[6] to watch our tongues, which speak hell into this world,[7] and not to become friends with this world lest we make ourselves enemies of God.[8]

Peter commands that we be alive to Christ and dead to temptations in this world[9] so that we might avoid the corruption that those evil desires cast upon us.[10]

Paul says that the world in all of its collective wisdom does not know God,[11] prefers lies that promote sin to Scripture, which demands repentance,[12] and parades foolish human teachers[13] who offer little more than arrogant and hollow speculation about life and God[14] that is merely false wisdom taught by Satan,[15] who is using the world to enslave people to sin and death[16] and stands condemned by God.[17]

Jesus came into the darkness of the world to show his love for us and to shine his light upon us.[18] And he has now sent us on reformission into the world to live as he lived.[19] By Jesus' empowering grace through the Holy Spirit in us, we can overcome the world.[20] Living in reformission therefore requires renewed thinking so that we will be shaped not by the patterns, values, and rhythms of this world but instead by Jesus' kingdom.[21] Faithfulness also requires that we wage our war against the world with the gospel weapons of grace, love, and truth, which the world does not have access to,[22] as we concern ourselves with being like Jesus, who has gone before us and now goes with us.[23]

All of this is to say that worldliness is a sin, and before we naively seek to be relevant to a dying world, we must realize the dangers before us and proceed with our eyes open and our hands ready for spiritual war. Tragically, I have seen many young pastors undertake reformission without a wise understanding of worldliness, pastors who, rather than converting lost people, were themselves converted and are no longer pastors but instead are adulterers, divorcees, alcoholics, perverts, homosexuals, feminists, and nut jobs. Most frightening of all are the pastors who have become worldly but remain pastors who preach a gospel that cannot save because it is little more than the hollow echo of a cursed world.

But while culture certainly contains elements of worldliness, the two are not synonymous. This point is incredibly significant, as many Christians have treated the two as synonyms, an error which by itself nearly kills reformission. Every culture has, in addition to worldliness, aspects of the good creation and the good image and likeness of God that people are made in. Because of this, there are elements in every culture that could be used to oppose God and his work on the earth but that are in and of themselves neutral and useable for either sin or worship. Examples include tasty food that could be used for either sinful gluttony or holy feasting, music that could be used for either idolatry or worship, and stylish clothing that could be used for either lust or beauty.

Last, it was God who created cultures at Babel when he scattered people across the earth with various languages. It was God who worked through cultures as varied as Babylon, Israel, Nineveh, and Egypt to redeem his people. It was God who came to the earth as a man who lived in a culture. And when Jesus ascended into heaven, it was God who enabled the disciples at Pentecost to proclaim the gospel in the languages and dialects of the many cultures that were assembled. In his kingdom, God promises that people from every race, culture, language, and nation will be present to worship him as their culture follows them into heaven. Automatically equating one's involvement in culture with worldliness not only is silly but also condemns the life of Jesus and compels his followers to be unlike him.

MYTH 2: GARBAGE IN, GARBAGE OUT

As a college freshman and a new Christian in the early 1990s, I had a Christian buddy tell me to throw all of my "secular" music out and get new "Christian" music. He reasoned that if I listened to non-Christian music, it would shape my mind and cause me to end up living like a non-Christian. While I doubted that listening to the Cure would compel me to wear eye shadow, I acquiesced and threw out all my CDs. I then bought "Christian" music that I did not like but tried to enjoy because I was told it was good for me, like cauliflower. I remember visiting my parents on a holiday once when someone (likely the teenage pothead miscreants from the neighborhood) broke into my 1969 Chevy truck and stole all of my Christian music. To this day I still crack a crooked smile every time I picture the look that must have come over the kids' faces when they popped my

Keith Green, Michael W. Smith, Steven Curtis Chapman, and Maranatha worship tapes into their stereo.

When the insurance money finally showed up and I had to replace my music, I was torn between buying the "secular" music that I enjoyed and the "Christian" music that I did not. After much prayer, I decided that God loved me and allowed my music to be stolen so that I could buy back the old albums that I enjoyed. And so I did, and as the pastor of a church filled with "secular" bands that hosts "secular" concerts, I have not had a regret since.

Meanwhile, my buddy's theology of "garbage in, garbage out" remains quite popular but has numerous flaws. First, there is no such thing as a pure culture untainted by sin and sinners, including Christian entertainment, which has had its share of scandalous behavior. Second, it is uncertain what distinguishes clean "Christian" and unclean "secular" entertainment forms and why Bibleman is so much better than Spiderman. Third, "garbage in, garbage out" theology assumes that if Christians see and hear sin up close, they will want to participate in it. But the fact is that sin looks good only from a distance; the closer you get to it, the more clearly you see it, the more sickening it becomes. Though I grew up in a neighborhood filled with drug use, I have never tried drugs in any form because seeing strung-out junkies walking around shaking and talking to themselves while going to the bathroom in their pants was more than enough to convince me that drugs are in no way fun or enjoyable.

Reformission requires discernment by God's people to filter all of the cultures they encounter, Christian and non-Christian, through a biblical and theological grid in order to cling to that which is good and reject that which is evil. As we engage culture, we must watch films, listen to music, read books, watch television, shop at stores, and engage in other activities as theologians and missionaries filled with wisdom and discernment, seeking to better grasp life in our Mars Hill. We do this so we can begin the transforming work of the gospel in our culture.

MYTH 3: BUILDERS, BOOMERS, AND BUSTERS

When the Baby Boom generation (named after the increase in births following the World Wars) came of age and broke with the lifestyle of their parents, the Builder generation (so named because they built our nation politically, spiritually, economically, militarily), the result was the creation of a generational identity.[24] The problem with this identity, like all generalizations, is that it accurately reflects only some people in that group. Not everyone spent the 1960s and 1970s unclean, unshaven, naked, and high, munching on vegetables while driving around the country in VW vans looking for God like a game of hippie hide-and-seek.

Baby Boomers	Busters/ Generation X	Millenials/ Generation Y
78 million people born 1946–1964	43 million people born 1965–1976	73 million people born 1977–1994.

I was born in 1970, and my generation has been given a few names, including Generation X by some Canadian guy because we apparently lack any identity and are the generational equivalent of a generic brand. We have also been called the Busters because we were supposed to be a broken generation, abandoned by our selfish hippie parents who got sobered up, shaved, and became yuppies who did not have the time to raise the kids they failed to abort. Some kids are already being called the Millenials, which is very sad because their name does not begin with a B, therefore ruining the entire marketing genius of this generational silliness that attempts to create a market where there is none, much like drawing arbitrary nonexistent lines on maps.

Evaluating people by their age group makes about as much sense as categorizing people by their height. Not all six-foot-tall old men are the same, and neither are all fifteen-year-old women. Even a cursory flip through the channels on your television or radio will prove that in our pluralistic and multicultural society, there is no simple way to break people into groups by any factor, including age.

Christians have fallen into the same trap, starting different services at their churches and hiring a pastor who is the same age as the group the services are supposed to be reaching. We must dig deeper into our understanding of the people we are seeking to reach than simply noting their age. People are highly complex, and any attempt to divide them by something as arbitrary as age is naive, silly, and doomed to fail.

How smart would it be to have three church services targeting people according to their height? The first service would be for people under five feet tall, the second for people between five and six feet tall, and the third for people over six feet tall. And how wise would it be for each service to have a different pastor carefully selected by his height, and worship music that incorporated a lot of prooftext verses about height (lots of songs about Zacchaeus for the first service, and lots of songs about the Nephthalim for the third)? Reformission requires that God's people pay more attention to the particular people in their culture than to the many books on generational theory written by self-appointed experts who, in the end, are speaking at best of only a narrow, white, suburban slice of the generational pie.

Now that we have some of our theology of culture in order, we are ready to follow in Paul's footsteps and walk around our Athens searching for reformission clues.

➲ REDEEMING:
THE ART OF BEING IN EXILE

God promised Abraham that his descendants would be blessed in order to be a blessing to the nations and cultures of the earth. We, his spiritual offspring, are likewise called to the same task by Jesus' marching orders in the Great Commission. This all seems very reasonable until we notice the manner in which God has often fulfilled this mandate. Historically, God has sent his people into exile so that they at least in part could be about reformission. Throughout history, God has sent his people into captivity in godless foreign cultures such as Babylon (Jer. 29:4), where they were forced to cross cultures and bring the knowledge of God to people they had previously avoided, whether they liked it or not.

This is precisely what happened, for example, to Daniel, who was born into an affluent Jewish home in Judah and was well bred, well fed, and well read. As a young man, likely a teen, he was taken into exile in Babylon against his will, but under the sovereign hand of God. Babylon was a godless and wicked nation, which is why the Rolling Stones named an album after it. Babylon was ruled by King Nebuchadnezzar, who attacked Israel, plundered God's temple, and used the stolen sacred items in his own temple to worship false gods.

At first glance, young Daniel appears to be a classic limp-wristed theologically liberal Christian who was happy to blend the biblical truth with Babylonian paganism in an effort to avoid conflict. He was valedictorian of the famed Babylonian Marilyn Manson Academy and graduated with straight A's in witchcraft, sorcery, astrology, magic, dream interpretation, divination, and the occult. Daniel was also buddies with, and an employee of, the Hitleresque kings in Babylon, whom he loved and served faithfully, ultimately becoming both a trusted advisor and key political leader in Babylon. Daniel's name, which was a tribute to a son of David and a priest who is mentioned in the Scriptures, was changed to the Babylonian name Belteshazzar, likely a tribute to a pagan Babylonian god. At first glance, Daniel's resume in no way resembles a godly young man's and would likely get him kicked out of most Christian high schools today.

At second glance, however, young Daniel appears to have completely separated himself from Babylonian paganism like a dogmatic Bible-thumping fundamentalist. Daniel refused to bow down to the false gods and idols of Babylon. He refused to stop praying to and worshiping his God alone. He refused to eat the king's food. He refused to refer to himself by the pagan name given to him, thereby forbidding Babylon to define his identity. And as he walked with his accountability group of godly friends, Daniel preferred death by lion mauling and fire to violating his conscience and the Scriptures.

In Daniel, we see the tension of reformissionaries who seek to be faithful to God in the time and place in which he has sent them into exile. Daniel was very helpful to the king and the Babylonians yet clearly told him that the king was a sinful enemy of God, needing to repent of his ways and trust the one true God. Daniel was as keenly aware as anyone of the sinfulness of Babylonian culture, and though he was immersed in that culture, he in no way endorsed or participated in its worldly elements. Daniel was recognized as a capable and skilled man, yet he continually and humbly attributed all of his wisdom and insight to his God, a fact that even the king came to learn. And despite his young age and difficult task, Daniel managed to glorify God while proclaiming and living the truth in a way that was both faithful to God and accessible to Babylon.

Do you spot the parallels to our situation? God desires to bless all nations and cultures of the earth through us, and so he has sent us into exile in places and among peoples no less strange or lost than the Babylonians. I would never have chosen Seattle as my place of ministry because it is one of the most politically liberal, expensive yet uncharitable, and least churched yet most self-righteous cities in the nation. But as Paul said on Mars Hill, it is ultimately God who has chosen my birthday and address, placing me in Seattle today (Acts 17:26). Likewise, where you live is a place of Babylonian exile where God has placed you to be about reformission. And it is incumbent upon you to be wise, faithful, and fruitful, like Daniel was, so that the gospel can take root in your Babylonian soil.

➲ REFLECTING:
REFORMISSION QUESTIONS

To make sure we move from the theoretical to the practical, let me suggest that you consider undertaking a one-week research project along with some Christian friends. If you are part of a small group, you might want to make a mutual commitment to try this. Or you may wish to do this as a family unit. Here are the four parts to this cultural-immersion project:

1. Try shopping at a new grocery store, reading magazines (especially their ads) you would never pick up (middle-aged male plumbers could read *Cosmo Girl*), listening to new music (Christian-pop fans would do well to tune in to the hardcore station), listening to new teachers (Christian-radio fans should tune in to a sexual talk program like Tom Leykis or Howard Stern), and watching a movie you normally would not.

2. During the week, make an effort to learn from the people whom you encounter in public settings, such as the bank teller or grocery store clerk. Simply ask them what they've learned about people after interacting with so many. You will find that they are a wealth of insight.

3. Most important, speak with lost people who are not like you, not for the purpose of converting them but rather for the purpose of learning what life is like for them in their culture.

4. After you have undergone your reformission refocus and have returned to your normal routine, ask the following questions about your culture, including your Christian culture. If you are reading this book as part of a group experience, your group may find it helpful to share your answers to these questions.

   a. Where do people spend their time and money?
   b. What do people do during their free time?

c. What do they fear?

d. What do they dream about?

e. Where do they shop?

f. What cultural experiences do they value?

g. What are the most painful experiences they have had?

h. What music do they listen to?

i. What film and television do they watch?

j. What do they find humorous?

k. In what ways are they self-righteous?

l. What do they read?

m. What is their spirituality?

n. Whom do they trust? Why?

o. What do they think about the gospel?

p. What sins will the gospel first confront and then heal for these people?

REFORMISSION INTERVIEW WITH TIM OTTLEY
Rocking for the Lamb

1. **What is your name?**

   Tim Ottley

2. **What is your age?**

   30

3. **Do you consider yourself to be a Christian?**

   Yes

4. **What is your vocation?**

   I am a band manager. I oversee the daily operations of the band and make sure everything gets done. I don't do everything myself, but I make sure that we hire the right people for each job and that each of them does a good job.

5. **What bands have you promoted?**

   I have worked with a variety of bands. I got my start in Nashville with a label called Tattoo, where I worked with the Choir and Common Children. From there I spent several years on the road and worked with various bands, finally finding a home with POD. I now work in their management office, where I also work with Blindside and Year of the Rabbit.

6. **How have people responded to Christians in the musical mainstream?**

   I think the idea of crossing over is an old issue, and I think it is more symptomatic of the lack of vision most bands show about their career. I think the problem lies in the fact that when people start their band, they don't give enough thought to whether this band should be in the Christian scene or work in the general market. I have certainly worked with bands who were in the

Christian music industry who had no business being there. They didn't want to minister to other Christians. It just happened that they got offered a deal with a Christian label. They then wanted to cross over to where they should have started.

So I guess that is all to say that I would hope for Christians that they would spend more time early in the band's development deciding what their mission field is. I think the general market labels are simply looking to make money and have a hit, so their focus is not about message or mission; it is about dollars. There is certainly interest in a lot of the Christian bands right now from the mainstream labels, given the success that some of these bands have had over the last few years.

7. Why are Christian artists moving farther into the mainstream?

Well, I think the fact that there is more money and more celebrity on offer doesn't hurt. That said, I certainly think there are artistic reasons. Christian music is a genre defined, unlike any other, by the beliefs of the musicians. But that doesn't limit the music that various artists will want to make. But the Christian music industry has to have some pretty well-defined  boundaries to survive. I think there are restrictions in terms of both musical and lyrical content that true artists would wish to be free of. That said, I want to restate that I think it is an issue of where you feel called to minister. For the artists I work with, they feel called to minister outside of the Christian industry for both artistic and spiritual reasons. I think there are plenty of great bands inside of the Christian industry who are very happy and indeed greatly blessed because that is where they have been called to be.

8. Why is the mainstream embracing Christian artists?

Well, I think the mainstream industry is embracing them because they are reaping financial rewards. Which is probably also the best explanation for why non-Christian corporations bought up all of the Christian record labels. It is still like any business, and it always comes down to the bottom line. But I think that there is  also an element in which God is using this music to speak to a world in pain. Certainly in this country of the last few years, people have turned to more positive and uplifting music because of all they see around them. The heart of man will always seek God; there is only one thing that can fill the emptiness and hopelessness we all feel. And I know there is money and fame at issue and we live in a cynical world that manipulates music and art to make money. But I know that this God-inspired music is touching peoples' hearts and bringing true hope. The world will stand in the way of that and the Devil will do what he can to make us ineffective, but God will always find a way to work and bring true hope. As an aside, I would like to say that I hope that people pray for my bands and for me. I know we stand in a difficult place and that at any moment we could get it wrong and distort the way in which people see God through us. We certainly face criticism often for not doing enough. Often people want us to do their job for them. It isn't the job of my band to preach the gospel to your friend you brought to the show or gave a CD to. It is your job; God called you to do it. We play music, and hopefully people feel better when we are done.

Chapter Six

THE SIN OF LIGHT BEER

How Syncretism and Sectarianism
Undermine Reformission

M y first car, a 1956 Chevy, had only sixty thousand miles on it. I owned it for a few years before foolishly selling it because it had four doors and I did not think it was cool enough for me. In high school, I used to drive the car to my summer job as a warehouse grunt unloading cargo containers on the Seattle waterfront. The commute was always a harrowing experience because I could not afford decent radial tires and the roads I traveled were covered with ruts from the many semis hauling cargo in and out of the warehouses. So I routinely got stuck in those ruts and found myself veering head-on into oncoming traffic nearly every day.

Similarly, the journey of the gospel from the time of Jesus to the present day has encountered a number of well-worn and dangerous ruts that are seemingly impossible to avoid. Because of their deadly nature, it is critical that we be aware of them and attempt to avoid traveling in them as much as possible. We want to avoid veering off of reformission.

➲ REMEMBERING:
THE PHARISEES, SADDUCEES, ZEALOTS, AND ESSENES

RUT 1: SEPARATING FROM CULTURE LIKE A PHARISEE
The Pharisees were a very zealous and conservative sectarian movement that Paul had been a part of prior to his conversion. They were highly committed to getting back to the Scriptures and their brand of hard-line old-time religion. They developed a litany of laws to separate themselves from others in an effort to maintain their purity and righteousness by living in their own isolated culture. The Pharisees basically believed that they were good and clean before God, so they looked down on everyone else and conveniently overlooked their own sins and hypocrisy.

Isn't this same rut traveled in our day whenever something posing as the gospel emphasizes anything we must do for God over what God has done for us in Jesus? We also travel this rut whenever we impose man-made rules on people in the name of achieving holiness by avoiding sinners and hiding out in a Christian culture. We travel this rut whenever we hold a self-righteous and judgmental attitude that sees the sin in others but not in ourselves.

Sadly, many people despise Christianity because all they have known are arrogant, self-righteous, and judgmental people claiming to be Christians, who avoid them as if they were infected and do little more than yell at them to be moral when they should be explaining how to be redeemed. Flipping through a phone book once, I saw one such church advertising itself as "Separated" and "Reaching Out to Seattle," presumably much like a boxer reaches out to an opponent with a jab.

RUT 2: BLENDING INTO CULTURE LIKE A SADDUCEE

The Sadducees were a more culturally accommodating liberal movement than the Pharisees. Rather than pulling away from the dominant culture, they were happy to syncretize with it. Their compromise was so thorough that they even denied a future resurrection and the existence of angels and demons (Mark 12:18–27; Acts 23:8).

We travel this rut today whenever we don't take sin and Scripture seriously. We also travel this rut whenever being approved by a culture becomes more important than being faithful to God. Last, this well-worn rut eventually leads to a universalism in which every religion leads to salvation and in which there is little, if any, distinction between true and false gospels. In my city, this includes the churches that promote themselves as "open and affirming," which is Judas-speak for pro-sodomy.

RUT 3: RULING OVER CULTURE LIKE A ZEALOT

The Zealots pursued political power in an effort to forward their national and moral agendas by force and authority. They routinely mistook the kingdom of God for their kingdom and sought to usher it in by might. Today this form of Christianity exists in both the religious right and left. It's present wherever people are more interested in sermons about legislative politics than in sermons about sin and repentance, wherever people get more excited about elections than Easter, wherever more people sign political petitions than sign up to join a Bible study, and wherever people believe that if we simply elect more people like us, the world will be a wonderful place.

RUT 4: IGNORING CULTURE LIKE AN ESSENE

The Essenes were not concerned with being separated from the culture like the Pharisees, or with cultural relevance like the Sadducees, or with political power like the Zealots. Instead, they wanted to personally encounter God in spiritual experiences. To accomplish this, they withdrew from society, denied themselves pleasure, and lived free from distraction in monkish privacy so they could have mystical encounters with God. This form of Christianity exists wherever people seek out spiritual highs like a junkie needing a fix, wandering from church to church and event to event hoping to be touched by God through the latest anointed spiritual bartender who's serving up hundred-proof glasses of ditzy deity.

The problem with each of these ruts is that they are ways of seeking godliness, as we define it, rather than as God defines it. But the things that those who are stuck in them desire (holiness, cultural relevance, social transformation, spiritual experience) can't be brought about by legalism, liberalism, legislation, or lunacy; instead, they are the natural effects of faith in the powerful gospel and come from God alone to those who are about his reformission business.

➲ REPENTING:
SYNCRETISM AND SECTARIANISM

Now that we have identified the ruts we are most likely to get stuck in, we can, like a two-wheel-drive pickup in a snowbank, repent, get unstuck, and get back on the road to reformission.

While the four ruts seem to be different, they are in many ways alike. For example, both the Pharisees and Essenes are sectarians who don't go far enough into culture. And both the Sadduccees and Zealots are syncretists who go too far into the culture.

The popularity of syncretism and sectarianism, however, should not surprise us, because Jesus predicted they would come. Knowing that we were being sent into the world as he had been sent into the world, Jesus prayed to the Father, "I am coming to you now, but I say these things while I am still in the world, so that they may have the full measure of my joy within them. I have given them your word and the world has hated them, for they are not of the world any more than I am of the world. My prayer is not that you take them out of the world but that you protect them from the evil one. They are not of the world, even as I am not of it. Sanctify them by the truth; your word is truth. As you sent me into the world, I have sent them into the world" (John 17:13–18).

With his death quickly approaching, Jesus had nearly completed the work the Father had sent him to do. Jesus prayed that his death and resurrection would birth a full joy within us. This joy in Christ is the well from which reformission is drawn. This point is important because too often the evangelistic task of speaking about Jesus is promoted as a work or something we must do, rather than as an overflowing of joy within us that explodes out of us because we have met God in Christ. Jesus then prayed that we would live a reformission life of tension, holding the gospel in one hand and the culture in the other, furiously refusing to let go of either so that we might be simultaneously faithful to the text of Scripture and to the context of our ministry.

To let go of culture is fundamentalist sectarianism. Sectarianism is the huddling up of God's people to enjoy each other and Jesus without caring about anyone who is lost and dying outside of Christ. To justify themselves, sectarians will often quote 1 Thessalonians 5:22 from the King James Version, which poorly translates this verse to say that we are to avoid every appearance of evil, when the text actually says that we should avoid every kind of evil, which is a different matter altogether. Sectarianism inevitably leads to irrelevance and is unfaithful to Jesus' prayer that we not leave this sick and dying world that does not know him.

While sectarians may cling to the gospel for their personal piety, they hide their light under a bushel. And so the story of

Jesus stays at home with my family, with my church, and with my Christian friends because for us salvation is a place to end and not a place to begin. Eventually, sectarians become so dated and removed from people in the world that their churches are little more than museums dedicated to the past, with dumb reader boards outside that sound like silly telegraphs from an alien planet.

To let go of the gospel is liberal syncretism, which also leads to irrelevance. How? By rarely, if ever, speaking of sin and repentance in personal and not just institutional and systemic terms. Syncretism simply baptizes unscriptural beliefs in the name of limp-wrested relevance, social progress, being nice, and making a good nonjudgmental impression. Syncretism inevitably dissolves into a universalism in which God loves everyone, and will forgive everyone's sins and take everyone to heaven because he simply lacks the courage to judge anyone. Eventually, syncretists become less distinctively Christian in favor of an inoffensive spiritual mush. Visiting syncretistic churches is like entering a mutual admiration society in which people pat each other on the back for having a social conscience and nod in agreement through sermons that sound like sappy greeting cards strung together to make us feel like we just got a divine back rub while doing aromatherapy, drinking herbal tea, and listening to taped sounds of running water.

The problem with both syncretism and sectarianism is that they deny the clear teaching of the Scriptures that the power of God unleashed through the gospel of Jesus Christ can transform anyone. Sectarians do not live by the necessary faith in the gospel and therefore believe that evil hearts and sinful actions and worldly social structures are more powerful than God, unable to be redeemed, and therefore are a waste of our energies because they are destined to be meat on God's grill anyway, so why bother? Likewise, syncretists do not live by the necessary faith in the gospel and therefore believe that the hearts of people aren't that bad, their actions aren't that sinful, and since people are doing the best they can, we can't expect any sort of radical transformation, and so we should simply bless them with a sentimental love.

Sectarians love God but fail to love their neighbor. Syncretists love their neighbor but fail to love God. Jesus expects us to love him and our neighbor (including our enemies) and says that if we fail to do so, we are no better than the godless pagans who love their drinking and strip-poker buddies (Matt. 5:43–47). To love our neighbors, we must meet them in their culture. To love our neighbors, we must call them to repent of sin and be transformed by Jesus.

➲ REDEEMING:
STOUT FAITH

To illustrate the pitfalls of syncretism and sectarianism, I want to unabashedly play plank and speck with the numerous Christians who consider alcohol consumption unfit for God's people and a measure of one's lack of piety. Prior to my conversion at age nineteen, my Christian buddies repeatedly told me that all alcohol consumption is a sin, even though I did not drink at that time. After my conversion, the same mantra was repeated to me, though I still did not drink. After I entered the ministry as a man of legal drinking age, the drum was again repeatedly beaten for me by well-meaning older pastors. So I never drank alcohol until I was thirty years of age. About that time, I was studying the Scriptures for a sermon about Jesus' first miracle of turning water into wine, as reported in John's gospel, a miracle that Jesus performed when he was about my age. My Bible study convicted me of my sin of abstinence from alcohol. So in repentance I drank a hard cider over lunch with our worship pastor.

Since that time, further studies of church history have led me to discover that a number of God's people down through the years have greatly enjoyed alcohol.[1] Saint Gall was a missionary to the Celts and a renowned brewer. After Charlemagne's reign, the church became Europe's exclusive brewer. When a young woman was preparing for marriage, her church brewed a special bridal ale, from which we derive our word *bridal*. Pastor John Calvin's annual salary package included upwards of 250 gallons of wine to be enjoyed by him and his guests. Martin Luther once wrote of the Reformation, "While I sat still and drank beer with Philip and Amsdorf, God dealt the papacy a mighty blow."[2] Luther's wife Catherine was a skilled brewer, and his love letters to her when they were apart lamented his inability to drink her beer. When the Puritan's landed at Plymouth Rock, the first permanent building they erected was a brewery.

Tragically, as feminism grew in America around the turn of the twentieth century, the women's suffrage and prohibition movements, which were the results of a feminine piety that came to dominate the church, also flourished. This all occurred as more women became pastors and the church became more feminine. At the same time, some denominations even began to condemn alcohol as sinful. In 1869, Methodist pastor Dr. Thomas Welch created the very "Christian" grape juice (Welch's) to replace communion wine. Consequently, many churches no longer offered communion wine, though it is what Jesus had at the Last Supper. The marriage of Christianity and feminism helped to create a dry nation that put out of business all but the largest brewers, who were able to survive on near beer (beer without the alcohol, which is nowhere near beer) and root beer. This horror explains why today American beer is largely mass produced, watered down, light on calories, and feminine compared with rich, dark, heavy, and more "biblical" European beers.

Thankfully, the resurgence of microbrewing in the United States is helping to overcome the great loss and to resurrect the art of brewing. I personally long for the return to the glory days of Christian pubs where God's men gather to drink beer and talk theology. If anyone should take me up on this suggestion, I would offer the following as possible brand names for your brews: Lord's Lager, Holy Hefeweizen, Pastor's Porter, Allelulia Ale, Saintly Stout, and Lucifer's Light.

In saying this, I fully expect that it raises questions for readers who, without searching the Scriptures on the matter, may have simply assumed that alcohol consumption and love for Jesus are mutually exclusive. So I'll briefly address the common arguments against alcohol consumption. But let me first mention some points on which all Bible-believing Christians agree.

Biblical Prohibitions against Drunkenness

- Drunkenness is a sin (Deut. 21:20; Eccl. 10:17; Luke 12:45; 21:34; Rom. 13:13; 1 Cor. 5:11; Eph. 5:18; 1 Peter 4:3).
- No priest was to drink alcohol while performing his duties (Lev. 10:9; Ezek. 44:21), though he could consume while not working (Num. 18:12, 27, 30).
- No king was to drink while judging law (Prov. 31:4–5).
- An elder or pastor cannot be a drunkard (1 Tim. 3:3; Titus 1:7).
- No drunkard will inherit the kingdom of God (1 Cor. 6:10; Gal. 5:21).

Biblical Problems Caused by Drunkenness

- incest (Gen. 19:32–35)
- violence (Prov. 4:17)
- adultery (Rev. 17:2)
- mockery and brawling (Prov. 20:1)
- poverty (Prov. 21:17)
- late night and early morning drinking (Isa. 5:11–12)
- hallucinations (Isa. 28:7)

- legendary antics (Isa. 5:22)
- murder (2 Sam. 11:13–15)
- gluttony and poverty (Prov. 23:20–21)
- vomiting (Jer. 25:27; 48:26; Isa. 19:14)
- staggering (Jer. 25:27; Ps. 107:27; Job 12:25)
- madness (Jer. 51:7)
- loudness combined with laughter and then prolonged sleep (Jer. 51:39)
- nakedness (Hab. 2:15; Lam. 4:21)
- sloth (Joel 1:5)
- escapism (Hos. 4:11)
- depression (Luke 21:34)
- staying up to party all night (1 Thess. 5:7)

All Bible-believing Christians agree that drunkenness is a sin that causes a life of misery. In addition, Christians are to obey their government in regard to alcohol consumption, which means that such things as underage drinking in America are sinful (Rom. 13:1–7).

But in an effort to prohibit God's people from all alcohol consumption, some Christians argue that terms such as *new wine* and *mixed wine* in the Bible refer to nonalcoholic wine. Curiously, the same people who often argue that when the Bible says "wine," it does not mean wine (what else could it mean, hubcap?) are also the most strenuous proponents of the inerrancy and truth of God's Word. But according to Scripture, new wine can still intoxicate, and mixed wine refers to special wines made by mixing various wines, sometimes with spices, and does not refer to wine cut with water.[3] The only time such a practice is mentioned in the Bible is in regard to sinful merchants who cut wine with water to rob customers.[4] When God refers to pouring out his mixed wine on his enemies, he does not mean he will dilute justice.[5] And finally, the Bible does speak of grape juice,[6] and so if God meant to speak of nonalcoholic wine, he would have said grape juice to avoid confusion.

THREE POSITIONS ON DRINKING

In his well-argued book *God Gave Wine,* Kenneth Gentry Jr. describes three positions on alcohol common among Bible-believing Christians.[7] His work is particularly helpful because while he argues for the biblical freedom of God's people to consume alcohol in moderation, he himself does not consume alcohol, and therefore he is arguing from pure motives, concerned only with the truth.

First, *prohibitionists* wrongly teach that all drinking is a sin and that alcohol itself is an evil. This position is untenable because the Bible teaches that God makes "wine that gladdens the heart of man" (Ps. 104:14–15), because Scripture is clear that Jesus' first miracle was creating over one hundred gallons of wine at a wedding party, and because Jesus ate enough food and drank enough alcohol to be falsely accused of gluttony and drunkenness.[8] So if alcohol is inherently evil, then God is evil because he makes it, and Jesus is sinful because he drank it. At the risk of pointing out the obvious, isn't it a terrible thing for us to try to be holier than Jesus by not drinking?

Second, *abstentionists* wrongly teach that drinking is not sinful but that all Christians should avoid drinking out of love for others and a desire not to cause anyone to stumble. Yes, Christians should avoid drinking in the presence of others who are unable to practice moderation and self-control.[9] But it is unreasonable to demand that all Christians abstain from all alcohol. The Bible teaches that God gave wine to his people even though they used it to worship the pagan god Baal.[10] Jesus drank alcohol even though there were undoubtedly people in his day who were alcoholics.[11] Paul says that only a demon would compel Bible teachers to forbid things that God made good[12] and that drinking alcohol can be done in a way that glorifies God.[13]

Third, *moderationists* rightly teach that drinking is not a sin and that each person must let Christian conscience guide them without judging others. This position is both reasonable and biblical because wine itself is neutral and can be used in both good and bad ways.[14] When used in a right and redeemed way, alcohol is a gift from God to be drunk with gladness, particularly when feasting.[15] When used in this way, feasting and drinking are foretastes of the kingdom, which will include new wine.[16] This also explains why in Scripture a lack of wine reflects the absence of joy.[17]

Biblical Occasions to Drink Alcohol in Moderation

- celebration (Gen. 14:17–20)
- the Lord's Supper (Matt. 26:29; Mark 14:25; Luke 22:18)
- medicinal purposes (Prov. 31:6; 1 Tim. 5:23)
- worship (Exod. 29:40; Num. 28:14; Matt. 26:27; 1 Cor. 11:25–26).
- thanksgiving to God (Prov. 3:9–10)
- happiness (Deut. 14:26)

WHY DOES THIS MATTER?

Now that we have established a flexible theology of alcohol that is more reasonable than many theologians', some readers may be asking, "Why does all of this matter?" It matters because alcohol is a very real example of the pitfalls of syncretism and sectarianism. Prohibition began as a syncretistic liberalism that took away alcohol and the Christian freedom to drink. This happened because churches aligned themselves with a non-Christian feminism that attempted to eliminate the pub as a gathering place for men to do theology, politics, and business. This syncretism undermined the clear teachings of Scripture in an effort to fabricate a theology that supported its cultural form of morality.[18]

Over time the prohibitionist mindset became so entrenched in evangelical and fundamentalist thinking that it is now a sectarian belief intended to keep God's people out of the pubs, clubs, and dinner parties where sinners gather to make friendships and memories — the very places where Jesus was often found. Heresy happens when the truth is taken too far, as is the case with drunkenness, and or is not taken far enough, as is the case with prohibition. Confusion about the gospel is truly at the root of this issue. While we are called to abstain from sin, that does not mean that we must abstain from culture to do so.

Martin Luther poked fun at the logical conclusion of this illogical thinking, saying, "Do you suppose that abuses are eliminated by destroying the object which is abused? Men can go wrong with wine and women. Shall we then prohibit and abolish women?"[19] His humorous argument makes the point well. Men sin with women, but we should not abolish women. People worship rock stars, but we should not abolish music. People worship food, but we should not abolish grocery stores.

This truth was clearly reinforced in my mind during a conversation with a conservative Jewish rabbi who explained to me his pride in being part of "the world's most organized religion." He explained the lists of rules intended to insulate his people from the dark and dying culture around them. He said that their religious meetings were in Hebrew and that they did not attempt to convert anyone because to do so would require his people to get involved in the culture. To stay holy, they abstained from the culture as much as possible, because sin is caught from infected people, just like a cold. When I asked him about the benefits of his faith, he explained that he and his people were basically better than everyone else because they obeyed man-made rules that quarantined them from sinners. Though I was grieved by the depth of his blindness and self-righteousness, I admit I was impressed by the consistency of his thinking. Tragically, he is leading a fools' parade of nice virgins who never drink, cuss, or watch a dirty movie but are skipping into hell because they don't love Jesus.

Here's what I'd like you to remember from this chapter: reformission is not about abstention; it is about redemption.

We must throw ourselves into the culture so that all that God made good is taken back and used in a way that glorifies him. Our goal is not to avoid drinking, singing, working, playing, eating, lovemaking, and the like. Instead, our goal must be to redeem those things through the power of the gospel so that they are used rightly according to Scripture, bringing God glory and his people a satisfied joy.

This matter is of urgent importance. The transition from a modern to a postmodern world has created a widening and increasingly angry division between Christians as to what a faithful witness looks like. Therefore, in the next chapter, I will critique both modern and postmodern cultures to encourage you to see them as equally lost and godless but not beyond the transforming power of the gospel and reformission.

⟳ REFLECTING:
REFORMISSION QUESTIONS

1. Which of the following ruts are you most likely to fall into? Why?
   a. A Pharisee who avoids culture.
   b. A Sadducee who compromises too much and accommodates culture.
   c. A Zealot who hopes to rule over culture through politics and power.
   d. An Essene who ignores culture in favor of religious experiences.
2. In what ways have you gone too far into the culture and compromised your conscience or Christian witness?
3. In what ways have you not gone far enough into the culture and missed opportunities for evangelism and ministry?

REFORMISSION INTERVIEW WITH MIKE HALE
Protestant Pubs

1. **What is your name?**

   Mike Hale

2. **Do you consider yourself to be a Christian?**

   Yes

3. **What is your age?**

   59

4. **What is your vocation?**

   I am the founder and president of Hales Ales Brewery.

5. **Name some famous brewers and pubs in the history of the church.**

   I have no knowledge of famous brewers or pubs in the history of the church.

6. **Why did you open your pub?**

   I started the Brewery in 1983, and I came to know the Lord Jesus in 1986.

7. **How will your pub contribute to the progress of the gospel?**

   I am unclear as to how the pub will contribute to the advancement of the gospel. I do witness to my employees and customers as the Spirit gives me openings, and my wife and I pray for them and the building most every day, generally and by name as the Spirit leads. Also, I am more and more convinced that the prohibition of drink by well-meaning Christians is a manifestation of the religious spirit as a substitution for the cross of Christ — you know, substitutions of our own works of righteousness to earn salvation. My presence here has led many Christians to rethink

this position. On a more personal note, this job is teaching me humility, which is leading to more gentleness, patience, longsuffering, and the ability to love more, if very slowly.

8. Do you serve light beer?

We do not serve light beer because it doesn't taste very good. Our role is to make the best beer we can.

9. How have people reacted to your owning a pub?

Many of my fellow Christians felt being a brewer or even a drinker of beer was a problem, but it seemed to me that leaving my company, which was dependent on me, would be irresponsible and not a good witness. After much study and seeking of godly men's opinions, I felt confirmed in that decision. Among other Scriptures was the one about staying in your circumstance until the Lord changes it for you. I have given the Lord every opportunity to pull me from this job, but he has kept me here, most recently in a dramatic way. Long story. Most people are surprised that a Christian would brew beer or own a pub.

10. Why do many Christians see drinking as incongruent with faith?

This flows from the historic position of American Christians. Most, when giving it some thought and study, conclude it is better than banking or lawyering. Just kidding, but many bankers and lawyers have confessed reservations about their professions to me. I have concluded that Jesus is much more concerned about who we are than what we do.

11. How would you respond to the charge that you are encouraging alcoholism?

Encouraging alcoholism is the most serious consideration I have had.

Along with this is concern for ordinary drunkenness or even overindulgence. I have concluded that this is a personal choice for each individual. The Christian alcoholics I have spoken with blame not the beer they drank but themselves for drinking too much of it. I have been unable to find evidence in my own experience or from my friends' experience that drinking is habit-forming or addictive in and of itself.

With regard to harm to a fetus, my mother drank during her pregnancy, as did most mothers in that era, without undue harm. I don't believe that moderate drinking is any threat to the unborn. Now abortion, that is a threat.

There are many medical studies showing that moderate drinking of any type of alcohol is beneficial to the heart, mind, and body. I would, however, restrict unsupervised drinking, or for that matter unsupervised driving, to the age of thirty. I don't encourage alcoholism, not by example and not by word. In my pub, and in most pubs, by law we must remove the drink of anyone who appears intoxicated and refuse them further service.

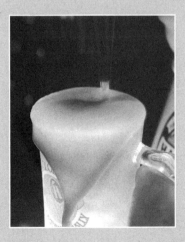

I don't believe alcohol to be a harmful substance but rather a blessing. But if the Lord chooses to remove me from here and give me a more reputable service to perform, I would be pleased. But I am not called to please men but rather him who has sent me. My mission is to discern his will and to follow it, and I do my best.

Chapter Seven

POSTMODERN PANDEMONIUM

Defeating the New Demons

➲ REMEMBERING:
THE CULTURAL MANDATE

It was the middle of the night, and my family and I were sleeping soundly in our beds when I was awakened by a distraught person banging on our front door and yelling. I leaped from my bed and told my wife to grab our children and lock herself in our bedroom, where she could hide and call the police. Ordering her not to open the bedroom door for any reason, I grabbed my handgun and took position at the bottom of our stairs, between our front door and my family, praying that I would not need to kill this person and then have to preach at the funeral. Fortunately, the police arrived before tensions escalated out of control. Unfortunately, this was not the first time such a thing had happened to my family. We had been harassed by demons, people, and demon-possessed people on more than one occasion.

My heart was racing so fast I laid awake for the rest of the night. I was filled with longing for the coming of King Jesus and his kingdom. After that day comes, we will not need locks on our homes, police officers, 911, or handguns and we will not fear, because sin and sinners will be no more.

Today, however, is not the end but the middle of history. Today, our eyes peer into the kingdom of heaven as we long for its coming, while our feet plod thorough the mud of the cultures on the earth.

While we are here, we are supposed to be cultivating a culture like the kingdom. In his book *Re-visioning Mission,* Richard Cote writes, "The word 'culture' derives its semantic origin from the Latin *cultura,* which initially referred to the cultivation of the soil and then by extension to the cultivation of the mind and spirit.... It embraces all aspects of human life in a given society: its values, beliefs, customs, forms of knowledge and art, etc. It is no longer an 'elitist' concept of the educated but one that applies to every individual and to all peoples."[1] Culture is not something that God's reformission people are merely to participate in; it is also something we are to cultivate, or plow, by living for the kingdom of heaven among the cultures of earth.[2]

In the first two chapters of Genesis, we see the elements of this kingdom culture. They include living in harmonious dignity with God and creation, blessing, feasting, masculinity and femininity, goodness, wisdom, work, marriage, song, lovemaking, and lots of children who honor their moms and dads to the glory of their God. This poetic vision is so holy, other, and different from our world that it requires great faith for us to believe that the redemption of our culture is possible.

⟳ REPENTING:
MODERNITY AND POSTMODERNITY

Because the kingdom is our model, we must be wary of every generation's tendency to tout a "new" culture to replace the kingdom. A case in point is the present-day postmodern bandwagon.

What can we say about postmodernism?

First, postmodernism is basically a philosophical junk drawer in which people toss anything and everything they cannot make sense of. If you ask four philosophers what postmodernity is, you will get five answers.

Second, postmodernity is not actually that new, as demonstrated by the fact that philosopher Huston Smith wrote about life on the other side of postmodernity in his 1982 book *Beyond the Postmodern Mind*.[3]

Third, even a cursory reading of Ecclesiastes shows that culture is a stationary bike that each generation climbs on in hopes of getting somewhere only to die and fall off so that the new young stud can take his turn peddling and, like a fool, make pronouncements about his progress. We would be wise to see postmodernity as simply the new guy on the old bike and not mistake cultural change for kingdom progress.

Fourth, postmodern culture is not something we should ignore, oppose, or embrace; rather, it is simply another culture that we should seek to redeem and transform by the power of the gospel. Indeed, culture is an old whore, and modernity and postmodernity are simply her old and new dresses.

Part of the confusion comes from the fact that even defining postmodernism is a very unpostmodern thing to do. Nonetheless, I will attempt in the stream of consciousness that follows to take you on a journey through the emerging matrix of our world. Are you ready for the ride? Remember, this is not an academic treatment of the subject. Instead, I will write whatever comes to mind for a while and then stop, because anything more than that on this subject gives me a headache of Absalomic proportions.

The troubles began with the well-meaning Roman emperor Constantine, who took the faith of a ragtag group of persecuted also-rans and transformed it into a first-rate religion. In so doing, he wed state and church, and their bizarre freak-show child became known as Constantinianism, or what the founding fathers of America over a millennium later would call civil religion. The church and her kingdom experienced great favor and freedom within the confines of the kingdom of the emperor. Over time, it became vogue to be a Christian, to the degree that some present-day nations fund churches with tax dollars, and every president of the United States has claimed to follow Jesus and then commenced his term, and the systematic violation of most of Jesus' commands, with a public prayer from a highly trained professional. The religious right has so committed itself to revisionist history that it sells the myth that the founding fathers were all good Christian folks with minivans who attended fundamentalist churches and received the Constitution on tablets of stone from deist Thomas Jefferson, who encountered the triune god (slavery, deism, and rationalism) on the same grassy knoll from which Roman Catholic John F. Kennedy was later killed.

A little over a thousand years into this doomed marriage of church and state, Rene Descartes was commissioned by the now-wealthy church to create a defense of the Christian faith against the emerging academic elite, which dismissed church teaching as outdated and unfounded superstition. Not satisfied with God's defense of himself by saying that people who don't believe in him are fools (Ps. 14:1), Decartes decided to create a big bottom piece on which to construct his giant Jenga game of philosophical inquiry. And what was his bottom piece? Simply, "I think, therefore I am."

With the firing of this rationalist shot, the human relay marathon toward disenlightenment commenced, since the only thing that could now be trusted was the individual and his or her mind. Armed with the scientific method, the four-hundred-year marathon proceeded from scientific rationalism (we can trust only what the mind can prove through "objective" scientific testing) to deistic naturalism (the world is a closed system that runs like a machine according to laws that cannot be violated, even by God) to skepticism (since God and miracles cannot be proven by science and violate our natural laws, it is unreasonable to consider religion as anything more than good morals for social order) to atheism (God does not exist, or as Nietzsche saw it before he lost his mind, God is an outdated concept that we killed).

This handing off of the baton, along with the evolutionary myth that we are born good and are getting better all the time — thanks to education, science, and social engineering — resulted in the oppression of the less fit and the killing of those who resisted "progress." We also learned from the industrial, scientific, and technological revolutions that science is good for more than just creating television altars before which the entire family can be numbed into a vegetative state by sports, game shows, and *America's Funniest Home Videos of Modern, Highly Evolved, Well-Educated People Laughing at Other Modern, Highly Evolved, Well-Educated People Getting Kicked in the Groin.* Yes, we could build bombs and guns and kill the bad guys. And so we did. Subsequently, the twentieth century witnessed more bloodshed and groin shots than all of human history.

Convinced the race should be called off before the world ended, some postmodern philosophers decided to pull the bottom piece out from under Descartes' now-towering Jenga game. Men like Jacques Derrida, Michel Foucault, and Richard Rorty began building on the critiques of Wittgenstein, Hegel,

Kierkegaard, and Kant to raise objections against the modern project. Is the concept of rugged individualism a dangerous myth? Is the human mind entirely trustworthy? Is it possible that objectivity is not possible? Is not naturalism an unproven faith assumption? Is not the human condition evil and not good? Is it truly funny to watch men get kicked in the groin?

And so postmodernity began. Not as a unified system of thought or as a collective dream for the future but instead as a critique, a deconstruction of a project that had laid its foundation with Constantine and became a high rise with Descartes. Now that the bottom piece of the Jenga game is almost entirely kicked out, the Western church finds itself, for the first time since Constantine, being dragged from the center of power and influence like a spoiled kid throwing a fit on the floor because he doesn't want to leave the party.

By this time, the Western church, having been in bed with the king so long and having enoyed the benefits of his palace so greatly that the concept of leaving had become unthinkable, had lost any concept of missions from the margins. So now, kicked out of the palace and sent by God on a mission into the chaos of the collapsing world, the mighty and empowered people of God instead pack up their evangelical-fish-sticker-baptized minivans and head at breakneck speed to suburban and rural areas far away from sinners and their cities. There they can safely hawk Christian gifts, market Christian bands to disadvantaged kids whose parents never allowed them to watch MTV, and invite their friends into the ghetto and erect the walls. Occasionally they toss a moral hand grenade over the wall at abortion doctors and homos and call it evangelism, the good news of the loving and well-marketed Rambo-Christ. At the same time, the mainline liberal church, which had happily married itself to the spirit of the modern age rather than to Jesus, now finds herself a lonely widow too old and senile to know that the deep conversations she has over breakfast each morning are with an imaginary friend and not her groom, who has long since died.

Meanwhile, the world surfs the internet, forming a global nation. Information expands at a rate unparalleled in human history. Everyone is spiritual, and atheists are now passe. People know that they are sinful, but without the hope of the gospel, they fall into depression and run to shrinks and drug companies to help them cope. People long to connect in community as whole people, while the church remains a goofy collection of individual minds with very bad pop music. Filmmakers are the new preachers, telling spiritual parables to a listening world, while nutty, Christian, end-times-prophecy Kaczynskis throw books on the shelves and films into the theaters trying to predict when we'll get off the postmodern roller coaster. And the lost — precariously propped up by Viagra and Prozac — try to squeeze out ten minutes of semisanity in our breakneck, isolated, selfish, debt-ridden, sexually confused, and lonely world.

Welcome to the postmodern pandemonium with its demons.

Perhaps modernity and its lonely individualism, arrogant rationalism, judgmental skepticism, and atheism was a demon that needed to be cast out. But as Jesus taught, unless that demon is replaced with the Holy Spirit, we are in deep dung, because seven new demons will take its place. After spending some years speaking with pastors from around the nation, including arguably most of the important leaders in what has been dubbed the emerging church, I have seen seven troubling demons that have entered the American church and brought fatal wounds to those ministering on the cutting edge. As we trod through the mud of culture, we must avoid the traps set by these demons so that we will continue to be about kingdom business.

➲ REDEEMING:
FROM NEW DEMONS TO KINGDOM VALUES

DEMON 1: THE SKY FAIRY

Jesus is not a nice old man in a button-up cardigan sweater and loafers singing happy songs while loading everyone onto a trolly headed to the Neighborhood of Make-Believe to meet King Friday like some Mr. Rogers clone. That god is the neutered and limp-wristed popular Sky Fairy of pop culture that wants to bless everyone, does not care what you call him/her/it/they, never gets angry, and would never talk about sin or send anyone to hell. This mythical Sky Fairy is increasingly mistaken for Jesus, however, by many young pastors and Christians I have met who don't want the gospel to be the offensive and foolish stumbling block that it is. So they remake Jesus into a feathered-hair fairy in lavender tights and take the sword of revelation out of his hand, replacing it with a daisy.

Perhaps this phenomenon is best articulated by non-Christian and leading postmodern philosopher Richard Rorty, who teaches at Stanford University. Rorty says, "I'm delighted that Liberal theologians do their best to do what Pio Nono said shouldn't be done — try to accommodate Christianity to modern science, modern culture, and democratic society. If I were a Fundamentalist Christian, I'd be appalled by the wishy-washiness of their version of the Christian faith. But since I am a non-believer who is frightened of the barbarity of many Fundamentalist Christians (e.g., their homophobia), I welcome theological Liberalism. Maybe Liberal theologians will eventually produce a version of Christianity so wishy-washy that nobody will be interested in being a Christian anymore. If so, something will have been lost, but probably more will have been gained."[4]

When our goal becomes innovation rather than faithfulness, we inevitably become simply a new kind of heretic who has accommodated God and his gospel to the degree that, as Paul told the Corinthians, we have a different Jesus and a different gospel. Ours is an increasingly spiritual age, but God's people should in no way perceive this as an indication that lost people who believe in the Sky Fairy are any closer to the true God than the atheists of a previous generation were. As we work among cultures that value trendiness, we must not forget that the kingdom values timeless truths like sin, repentance, and faith that leads to good works.

DEMON 2: KEEPING IT REAL ... SINFUL

One of the most popular mantras chanted by young pastors who align themselves with postmodernity is that God's people need to be more real and authentic. In general, this is wise. A disingenuous faith is repugnant to believers and nonbelievers alike.

But because we are sinners, simply encouraging people to be who they are in the name of authenticity is dangerous because it can easily be taken as a license to sin without repentance. In the opening chapter of Romans, Paul says that people are prone to be real rather than repentant because they love to sin, which explains why Jesus told us to deny ourselves rather than to be ourselves.

This tragic fact has conveniently been ignored by many emerging church leaders ministering in the postmodern pandemonium. The list of young pastors who have been known to be fired from ministry for fornicating, committing adultery, frequenting strip clubs, and getting drunk is very troubling. When confronted, one such young pastor weakly argued that he was being authentic and muttered some misquote of Scripture about not judging people. As we work among cultures that value realness, we must not forget that the kingdom first values repentance.

DEMON 3: HERMENEUTICS OF THE DRAGON

In the opening chapter of his scathing rant to the Corinthians, Paul mocks the self-appointed wise philosophers of his day. What would he write if he were living in our day? Would he say postmodernity is just another pretentious philosophy destined for the dung heap of history?

Postmodernity is tough to pin down, though, because it changes the rules of hermeneutics but keeps the Bible. Some postmodern pastors keep the Bible but reduce it to a story lacking any authority over us, feeling free to play with the interpretation and meaning of particular texts. They do not believe in a singular truthful interpretation. They believe that the interpreter ultimately has authority over the text and can therefore use it as he or she pleases rather than submit to it.

While this dance may seem novel, it is as old as Eden. Satan first used this tactic on Adam and Eve, and later used it to tempt Jesus, by manipulating God's Word to change its meaning. In previous generations, the fight was over the inerrancy of Scripture. Today, the fight is over the authority and meaning of Scripture. Possibly the most astonishing examples that I have seen are the reinterpretation of Scripture so that Mary Magdalene was married to Jesus, and a seminary professor and friend who teaches Bible interpretation for a living but goes through wives like socks.

As we go about reformission among the cultures of the earth, we must not forget that Scripture speaks of itself as a sword, and that our enemy, the Dragon, continually seeks to run us through with that sword, as he did our first parents.

DEMON 4: FROM CREATION BACK TO EX NIHILO

Modernity was a great building project whose aim was to construct a utopian society to the glory of man, a project similar to the Tower of Babel. This pride, combined with the Darwinian myth of human progress, fueled the creation of nations, schools, institutions, organizations, religions, and denominations. The modern era was about constructing institutions to shape people who would help humanity.

But what the modern era overlooked was human sinfulness, and what it lacked was a transcendent vision of what sinners need to have better lives. So the modern project became a bloodbath. More people were killed in the twentieth century than in all of human history as competing visions fought for preeminence.

Weary of conflict and war, postmodernity is a negative reaction to modernity rather than a positive vision of a better alternative. In its simplest form, this is what the philosophers are calling deconstruction, which is an academic way of saying that some people, like little kids, enjoy breaking things by tearing them apart. But deconstruction is easier than construction, and deconstruction without a rebuilding plan leads to homelessness. Cultures, like homes, house people, and cultures unfit for residency need to be torn down like junk houses. But then an architect is needed to create a vision of something better or there will be a lot of people left homeless. This sense of homelessness pervades those who have undertaken to deconstruct God, Scripture, gender, sin, the meaning of life, and anything else they can find.

Christians, especially young Christian leaders, are often so influenced by all this postmodern whining that their faith becomes, in large part, defined by what they are against rather than what they are for. They will articulate with great passion that they are against megachurches and any and every type of Christianity they can find. But when you ask them what they are for, you are often met with blank stares, because they do not know. Sadly, this also explains why many of the Christian churches and ministries that have aligned themselves with postmodern thinking remain insular, small, critical, and negative, exchanging God's mission for cultural malaise.

Many of the critiques of modern Christianity are legitimate and desperately needed. Every movement of God to redeem a culture begins with frustration and as a reaction. But those reactions and frustrations are seasons that must be quickly passed through, like puberty, so that maturity, vision, mission, and the hope of the gospel can become the primary issues for God's people on reformission. We must remember to do more than critique the work of others; we must help cultivate a kingdom counterculture where we live.

DEMON 5: THE CUSTOMER IS ALWAYS EVIL

People are more likely to worship themselves than God, which is idolatry. This explains why we all long for the world to bend to our needs and why we become frustrated when someone or something does not work in our favor. This proclivity toward self-worship (also known as self-esteem, self-actualization, self-help, and self-fulfillment) is particularly dangerous when combined with the economic value that the market should provide whatever people think they need. The result is a gluttonous and spoiled culture, as the following statistics indicate.

- In ninety nations, people spend less each year than we in the United States spend on our garbage bags.[5]
- Each year more Americans declare bankruptcy than graduate from college.[6]
- We have twice as many malls as high schools.[7]
- We spend more on shoes, jewelry, and watches than on higher education.[8]
- Our supermarkets have 250 percent more items than they did twenty years ago.[9]
- Parents spend six hours shopping each week, and forty minutes playing with their children.[10]

- Only one-fourth of shoppers have a particular purchase in mind when they go to the mall.[11]
- Seventy percent of Americans visit a mall each week; that's more than visit houses of worship.[12]

The assumption that everyone is a customer to be marketed to is a great pitfall for those who proclaim the gospel, because we tend to cast God as a product, and as mainstream a product as possible. After all, scriptural teaching about the curse, death as the wages of sin, the flooding of the earth, the killing of Egyptian babies, the slaughter of perverts in Sodom and Gomorrah, and the fiery torments of hell is a tough sell even for the best of marketing firms.

Yet today everything from sex to Jesus is pimped, since some preachers have traded in prophecy for pandering. Meanwhile, people have become so seasoned from the years of direct mail, online pop-up ads, commercials, and the endless parade of advertising on everything from billboards to ball caps that they tend to view the church as just another business and the preacher as yet another huckster.

Businesses of all sorts shamelessly pander to felt needs, and customers love the benefits they reap from fierce competition. People often take the same approach to God when they "shop" for a new church that emphasizes their felt needs and offers more amenities for them to consume. They expect God and his church to play their game by assessing their felt needs, marketing to them with a good pitch from a winsome salesman, and providing spiritual goods and services that beat the competition down the street, whether it's a self-help guru or another religion or church. Churches that buy into this worship of humanity are prone to fashion their churches after malls, complete with departments or ministries for each family member in an effort to keep the shoppers happy.

People with this transaction mindset about God and church will even see ministry not as something they do with the spiritual gifts God has given them but rather as something that is done for them as a religious service by someone else. Consequently, churches pandering to this mindset are filled with consumers who take more than they give and with observers who watch more than they participate. At its extreme, some people will actually pick from the programs and offerings of the several churches and ministries they like best without giving time or service to any of them, all the while failing to see their selfishness.

In the modern church, catering to the consumer mindset meant creating large churches that preached a positive message focused on Jesus' resurrection victory. In the postmodern church, it means creating small churches that have a despairing message focused on Jesus' bloody suffering, have a more pessimistic attitude, and continue to meet people's felt needs, which have simply changed. But as we cultivate a counterculture, we must not forget that what people need most is to die to themselves and live for God. If we simply give people what they want, we will not be giving them what they need.

DEMON 6: THE PHOTOCOPY HERESY

The vast majority of isms, such as postmodernism and feminism, spring from the myth of egalitarianism, the silly notion that everyone is equal. Like all heresies, this one is half true. In one sense, everyone is equal because we are all made in the image and likeness of God. But the fact remains that some people are smarter than others, some people are nicer than others, some are more helpful than others, some are more hardworking, some more trustworthy, and some more gifted by God. The apex of folly is our culture's myth that everyone's opinion is of equal merit, and so we have Joe Uninformed calling in on talk radio to give his two cents, and attempts by nightly newscasters to get the opinions of regular people about issues concerning nations they cannot spell the name of or locate on a map.

In an effort to maintain equality, our culture has pursued a bland sameness, such as by erasing distinctions between males and females in the name of making people equal, as if difference necessarily translates into inequality. Michel Foucault, one of the patriarchs of postmodernity, was an active homosexual until his death from AIDS in 1984 at the age of fifty-seven.[13] Postmodern patriarch Richard Rorty was clear about the influences of his upbringing in a home which was closely tied to communism. These factors in large part explain the postmodern fascination with gender, class, race, and the ensuing effort to eradicate distinctions between people in the name of fairness and equality.

Theologically, a postmodern church addicted to egalitarianism is also marked by a confusion over gender issues, such as masculinity and femininity, and sexual issues, such as homosexuality and bisexuality, as well as by a peculiar commitment to making sure that everyone's voice is equally heard and everyone's input is equally considered, whether or not it is foolish, as if the church were one big internet chat room. Some churches have gone so far as to replace a preaching monologue from a recognized leader to a spiritual dialogue among a group of peers who refuse to acknowledge any leader in authority over them. This makes about as much sense as shooting your doctor and gathering with the other patients in his lobby to speculate about what is wrong with one another and randomly write out prescriptions for one another in the name of equality.

Tragically, this pursuit of a flat culture of bland sameness and silly equality has resulted in postmodern theologies that are seeking to diminish even God in an effort to make him

equal with us and more like us. An example would be open the-
ism, which teaches that God does not rule over history and
know the future but rather, like us, is trapped in history, striving
to create the future with us. Are we truly to believe that human
history is a buddy-cop movie in which we journey throughout
time fighting the world, the flesh, and the Devil with God,
whose hands are tied and fingers are crossed in hopes that the
good guys will win in the end? As we work among cultures that
despise hierarchy, we must remember the kingdom values of
children honoring their parents, wives respecting their husbands, Christians following the leadership of their pastors, and
churches submitting to Jesus, because the governments of
home and church belong to God and not the culture.

DEMON 7: THE HYPHENATED CHRISTIAN

Some experts think that postmoderns are simply a new kind of
Christian, like a Western or Eastern Christian. But many post-
modern Christians are so postmodern that their hyphenated
Christianity has in effect negated their Christianity, like a New
Age Christian or a Buddhist Christian.

The reason why postmodern Christianity is ineffective has
to do with authority and power. Postmoderns see scriptural
texts as means by which spiritual leaders exercise power over
people. And because of their suspicion of power and authority,
postmoderns who are consistent in their thinking reject any
authority beyond themselves, and they reject any claim to truth,
other than their truth claim that there is no such thing as a valid
truth claim. The problem is rarely a philosophical hang-up but
rather a stubbornly hard heart that receives truth as readily as
a large rock receives bullets.

The Bible claims to be a revelation from God that can be
understood only by God's bypassing our resistance and renew-
ing our hearts and minds to both know and love him and his

truth. Postmodern culture claims that revelation is not possible and that all we are left with is the speculation of competing interest groups who seek to impose their authority over us. Because of this, we have descended from the light of truth into the darkness of perspective.

As it became increasingly apparent that there would never be widespread agreement on the truth, it became more popular to speak of truths. Someone could believe that something is true yet wouldn't expect anyone else to agree.

But since we all have to live on the same planet and get along to some degree, it was soon discovered that allowing everyone to have their own truths made it difficult to build a society of united people. Consequently, values then became in vogue as a list of things that most people considered to be good and helpful to the building of the culture, values such as tolerance, freedom, and equality.

However, though these values helped to undergird our culture, some people persisted in having strong convictions. Thus, the idea of opinions was born. If people are passionate about something, such as Jesus' being the only means to salvation, their opinion is to be considered not truth, a truth, or even just a value that should be promoted but rather as simply a personal opinion that they should be careful to keep to themselves in the name of politeness and equality, because people who disagree with them are just as right as they are.

So the postmodern concept of perspective was born. Now, people who claim to know the truth or a truth or even have an opinion about most anything that matters are dismissed as only looking at things from their narrow and biased perspective, because after all, revelation does not exist; speculation is all we have, and who can trust mere perspective?

But as we work among cultures, we must never proclaim Jesus as God merely from our limited and biased perspective but rather as God and the King who rules over a kingdom that includes the cultures of the earth. And the view from his throne is not simply one of the many equally valid perspectives but truth. If we fail in this, hyphenated postmodern Christians will reject any singular interpretation of Scripture, arguing that it is just your perspective and that there are other perspectives, none of which are true, so we should be tolerant of all. They will reject any leadership and shun what they call "organized religion," preferring to have self-styled spiritual experiences. They will also shun any form of officially responsible leadership, making them bad parents, spouses, and church members. In addition, they will demand that the Bible be taught as a series of suggestions rather than commands, that ministry be facilitated rather than led, and that self-discovery be promoted over obedience to God.

And reformission will cease.

Now that we have investigated how to move through the mud of the modern and postmodern worlds, we can begin building a kingdom culture where we live. In the final chapter, I will share with you what this looks like at our church and will try to inspire you to pursue the dreams that God has given you for the place in which you live.

⮕ REFLECTING:
REFORMISSION QUESTIONS

1. Take the time, perhaps over the next few days or weeks, to read the gospel of John and circle each occurrence of the word *truth,* or a derivative thereof. What did you learn about truth? How does what John says about truth differ from what your local culture believes about truth?

2. Do you consider yourself to be more modern or postmodern? Why?

3. Which of the seven demons is most worrisome to you? Why?

4. Do you think any of the seven demons are compatible with Christianity? Why or why not?

REFORMISSION INTERVIEW WITH JENNY SCHNEIDER
Glued to the Tube

1. What is your name?
Jenny Schneider

2. Do you consider yourself to be a Christian?
Yes. I committed my life to Christ at the age of thirteen.

3. What is your age?
27

4. What is your vocation?
I work in Broadcast Standards for a major television network. My department monitors and edits prime-time and children's programming, network commercials, and so on for content. This is to ensure that in anything and everything on-air, there is nothing that our audience would be too offended by (sex, violence, language). We work with producers, advertisers, and animators at every phase of the production of their commercials or shows and monitor what they are writing or producing to broadcast on the network.

5. Why do you believe your vocation is an important part of your faith?
Being a Christian in the entertainment industry is definitely a challenge, but it is an important part of my faith because Jesus tells us in Matthew 5:16, "Let your light so shine before men, that they see your good works and glorify your Father in Heaven." I want my life to be a testimony of God's saving power, which ultimately brings him glory.

6. How has it been tough to do your job well and be a Christian?

The toughest part for me has been that I see, firsthand, what is allowed to air on network television. The trend today seems to be to see how far the envelope can be pushed or to take risks and gauge how much the audience can handle before they will protest.

7. How have people reacted to your job?

For the most part, Christians are encouraged when I tell them about my job because they know I am here representing Christ. As for non-Christians, most are respectful and accepting of my faith, since Hollywood is a very liberal place where the motto is "whatever works for you."

8. Why should Christians be involved in Hollywood?

As believers, we need to be involved in Hollywood because television and the media reach such a broad audience, and we cannot underestimate what God can accomplish through any medium. After all, Jesus went out, got involved with the people, and immersed himself in the culture of his day for the sake of reaching people with the gospel. How else will the entertainment industry be reached if Christians are not here, involved in their lives, even if it is only on a professional level?

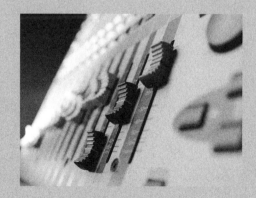

CONCLUSION

From Demons to Dreams:
Building a Kingdom Culture

This is the end of the book, and I'm supposed to go out with a bang, like the fireworks finale on the Fourth of July. But I'm sitting at home on a Saturday, which is supposed to be my day off, in my daddy chair drinking tea, wearing my pajamas, and trying, to no avail, to be profound. I am hoping that you will recommend this book to your friends and that I will become so important that I can do eccentric things like Prince and maybe one day change my name to a symbol because I have never liked the name Mark. My kids are in the playroom running around like midget demons arguing over crackers and juice with all the intensity of opponents and advocates of the death penalty at a state-sponsored execution. My lovely bride is making soup that smells good, and I am in a hurry because we have someone coming over and I need to shave so that I will look like an official pastor instead of a hobo.

The man who is coming over is a brand-new Christian. He is a photographer who was assigned to take pictures for a documentary on me and our church. When we first met, he told me to pretend he wasn't there as he followed me around, shooting photos of me doing the dishes, preaching, getting the mail, serving communion, and renting stupid action movies at the video store, which was weird because everyone there wondered why I had my own paparazzo. He stressed that he needed to be objective, but before long, reformission evangelism occurred, and he was eating with my family and becoming a friend who asked buckets of questions about life and God while we drove around in my 1978 Chevy truck. He asked me for a Bible, which he began reading, and last week God changed his heart. On Sunday, right before I preached, he came up to me, and I asked him if he needed to take more photos that day. He said that he had given his life to Jesus and was just going to church. That morning, I got to serve him communion. He's an amazing guy who has filmed for major media outlets some of the most horrific wars and evils in the world, from Haiti to Kosovo to Rwanda to Afghanistan. As we've talked, I've found he's pretty burned out trying to find hope in the cultures under the sun, and he longs for a kingdom culture.

Tomorrow, I get to stand on the large stage at our church and speak to a big crowd about Jesus and how one day he is coming back with a sickle in his hand to eliminate sin and sinners. Right before taking the stage, I will go to the bathroom, because for some reason I always have to pee before I preach, probably because I get nervous. My text is Revelation 14, and just this morning I was meditating on the fact that once the final angel is sent forth into the earth to proclaim the gospel to all people, the opportunity for repentance will cease, reformission will come to an end, and I will be out of a job. Honestly, I cannot wait for that day when I get to join the choir of worshipers, see the people who have passed from death to life, and sleep in every day because Jesus has things covered.

In the meantime, I have a lot of work to do where God has called me. My city is an absolute spiritual disaster. If Satan were in charge of it, I would assume it would look pretty much like it does right now, which leads me to believe that's exactly what is happening. The task of transforming this city seems completely overwhelming, and since we started our church seven years ago, I frequently have to remind myself that Jesus' tomb is empty, so that I don't lose hope and form a therapy group with Jim Beam, Jose Cuervo, and Johnnie Walker.

The problem with my pastoral job is that I don't really know what I'm doing. So I read every book I can find and I cling to the Bible like a kid who can't swim but somehow found a life preserver in the middle of the ocean. The principles I've shared with you in this book are things I've discovered while messing up, since I have a tendency to find landmines by stepping on them.

Often, I just want to be left alone or to start preaching sermons that sound like pithy statements strung together from fortune cookies and just cash my paycheck every week. But I can't help myself. Invariably, I see the needs of the culture and the condition of the church, and like the Hulk, my skin becomes green, my eyes bulge out of my head, and I lose the ability to speak in full sentences. So I just keep going and more people keep getting saved and more churches keep getting planted and I keep seeing more that needs to be done.

The only thing that gets me out of bed on Monday is the picture in Revelation of King Jesus on his throne ruling over all of creation, which is his kingdom. I've never seen what John saw, so I am forced to take his word for it. But because Jesus is in charge of everything, there is hope, even for my city. In closing, I want to show you what I'm up against as we seek to build our kingdom culture. I do this not to boast but rather because I want you to see what reformission looks like in practice. I don't expect you to do what we do, because you live somewhere else that is probably as messed up as where I live but in different ways. So you'll need to think through what you are up against there and what your kingdom culture would look like. The appendix at the end of this book may also help you to envision the future so that you can prepare for it.

Men in our kingdom culture. In Seattle, the young men are, generally, pathetic. They are unlikely to go to church, get married, have children, or do much of anything else that smacks of being responsible. But they are known to be highly skilled at smoking pot, masturbating, playing video games, playing air guitar, freeloading, and having sex with their insignificant others. However, the emerging-church massage-parlor antics of labyrinth-walking by candlelight will do little more than increase the pool of extras for television's *Will and Grace.* If there is any hope for a kingdom culture to be built in Seattle, getting the young men to undergo a complete cranial-rectal extraction is priority number one.

While the rest of the organizations in the city are busy trying to clean up the messes made by these young men, including unwed mothers, fatherless children, and crime, we focus our efforts on converting them and training them in what it means to be a godly man. So far our training on everything from how to study the Bible, get a job, invest money, buy a home, court a woman, brew beer, have good sex, and be a pastor-dad to their children has been very successful for hundreds of young men. We now have unmarried men buying homes in faith that one day God will give them a wife, and we have childless college men starting college funds in faith that one day God will give them a wife and children. We have a long way to go, but the building of our kingdom culture begins with building the men who will build that culture by building churches, families, and businesses. Therefore, in our kingdom culture, we take very seriously Paul's words that men are the glory of God (1 Cor. 11:7).

Sex in our kingdom culture. In our city, marriage, sex, and children are three unrelated issues. Young people live together and sleep together with no plans to get married or have children. And should a pregnancy occur, aborting the baby is assumed by many to be the only option. In our kingdom culture, we connect these three issues. We put prospective couples through a rigorous premarital process that clearly defines the biblical roles of husbands and wives. We average more than a wedding every week. We also value liberated marital sex and provide frank teaching on everything from why husbands enjoy oral sex to the different types of orgasms a wife can experience. In our kingdom culture, the marriage covenant is sacred and the marriage bed is sensual. We speak frankly, but not crassly, about sexuality because if our people do not get their information from the living waters of Scripture, their thirst will compel them to drink from the toilet of pornography and perversion.

Children in our kingdom culture. Our city is filled with young people who either are gay or are shacking up with the person they are dating. Consequently, our city has fewer children per capita than every American city except San Francisco. Many of these children have no father. To say that our city hates children may sound harsh, but in practice, it's a reality. In our kingdom culture, children are welcomed as a blessing from God because they will ensure that reformission continues well into the future. We value children not simply because they are cute or teach us life lessons but also because a reformission legacy matters. We believe that we should multiply and have lots of children, and then cultivate those children to live fruitful lives that include one day having lots of children who live fruitful lives.

Home in our kingdom culture. In our city, home building is a lost art because everyone works in the marketplace. In our kingdom culture, the home and the marketplace are equally important. While the husbands work in the marketplace, the wives build the home. Our home building includes helping people to buy a home and settle down rather than wandering from city to city. We offer training on buying a home and have church members who assist as realtors and mortgage brokers. One of our pastors even got his real-estate license so he could manage the home purchases of our people and give them their realtor's fees back to put toward their down payments. We encourage people to purchase homes large enough to have others live with them, either in a rental or gratis situation (often to help other people save enough money to buy their own homes), so that we have Christian community. We encourage our people to buy their homes with hospitality and ministry in mind so that they have enough space to host Bible studies and parties and to practice reformision evangelism.

Beauty in our kingdom culture. In our city, great value is placed on creativity and the arts. In our kingdom culture, we also hold these things in high regard and believe that one of God's attributes is beauty. We display paintings, photos, and works in other media for the sake of beauty and the encouragement of artists. We run an all-ages concert venue in which young people can enjoy non-Christian (and occasionally Christian) bands in a great room. We paint the walls of our homes and church because we worship God and not an orthodontist who only believes in sterile white surroundings. We write most of our worship music. We take aesthetics very seriously in everything from our building to our website. And our sound system is very important, since God cares about acoustics, and when he sings over us in the kingdom (Zeph. 3:17), we expect it to sound good.

Joy in our kingdom culture. In our kingdom culture, we laugh a great deal and embrace irony and sarcasm as gifts from our hilarious God. Jesus told us that the kingdom will be filled with joy, and so we make it a habit to take God very seriously and everything else very lightly. Some people misperceive our joy as triteness, but it is instead for us a demonstration of faith. Because our God rules over everything and is good, we are free to laugh, especially when times are tough. In our kingdom culture, good food, good drink, good friends, and good times filled with laughter stand in contrast to the worry, hurry, and busy of stressed and depressed people who do not trust God.

Practical theology in our kingdom culture. In our kingdom culture, we believe that claiming Jesus as Lord means that he rules over everything from our pots and pans to our genitals and car horns. As we read the Old Testament, we see that God talks about such things as why it is important to go to the bathroom in a hole, because otherwise people will step in it, and we believe that God truly cares about the minutiae of our lives. Consequently, in our kingdom culture, theology is intensely practical and connected to how we live every day as we work our jobs, clean our dishes, and brush our teeth to the glory of God. The Wisdom Literature contains some of our favorite biblical treasures.

Emerging leaders in our kingdom culture. Our city is very young and is dominated by the youth culture. In his day, Isaiah lamented that the youth culture was so domineering that it oppressed God's people (Isa. 3:12). Likewise, in our day, youthfulness is worshiped. You'll never see a middle-aged woman grace the cover of a Victoria's Secret catalog. The American concept of adolescence excuses immaturity among young people and welcomes rebellion and folly as rites of passage. In our kingdom culture, young people are identified not as adolescents but rather as Christians of whom Christian living is expected. We believe that because some of the greatest prophets and kings in the Bible were in their teens and early twenties, Christian maturity and leadership should be expected at a young age.

Church planting in our kingdom culture. Our city is one of the least churched in our nation, and our churches tend to be smaller and more theologically liberal than the national average. In addition, many of these churches are dead and dying because they are detached from both the Scriptures and culture. The situation is so bleak that even if God should stir the hearts of a fraction of the people in our city to attend church, there would not be enough seats for them. For those who could get a seat, it is questionable whether they would hear the gospel. In our kingdom culture, church planting is the logical outgrowth of reformission, since every culture and community needs vibrant churches to be the reformission base from which the gospel is taken into the culture. We give away one-tenth of our annual budget in order to help start churches wherever in the world God raises up a qualified leader to do reformission. We fund only nationals to plant churches, start orphanages, build schools, and do reformission, because we believe that every nation should have native Christians doing in their culture what we do in ours.

I pray that Seattle will no longer be known as one of the least-churched, least-married, most-perverted, and most-childless cities in our nation. I pray that Seattle will no longer be the national testing ground for godless political agendas and false gospels. I pray that so many people will have met Jesus and had their lives transformed by him that our businesses, governments, schools, homes, marriages, children, and churches would be holy, or different, because people had met God.

I pray that you and God's people in your culture would clearly see the opportunities for and obstacles to the gospel where you live. I pray that you and God's people would weep over the condition of your city. I pray that you and God's people would envision what your kingdom culture will be.

I pray that God would protect you from the world, the flesh, and the Devil, which conspire to thwart reformission. I pray that God would open to the gospel of grace the hearts of the lost people that you meet. I pray that God would get his glory, that your city would get its kingdom culture, and that you would get your joy.

Amen.

POSTSCRIPT

The words printed here are concepts. You must go through the experiences.

— Augustine

APPENDIX

Peering through Portals into Tomorrow

Regarding the future, a Chinese proverb says, "The person who does not worry about the future will shortly have worries about the present." Indeed, many of the present crises in the church and the culture are the result of the failure to anticipate the future and prepare for it. Also, many crises that the church and the culture might have suffered were averted because of foresight and prevention.

Discerning the future, however, is a highly subjective activity for everyone but our omniscient God and the prophets through whom he speaks. In 1893, journalist Junius Henri Browne said, "Law will be simplified. Lawyers will have diminished, and their fees will have been vastly curtailed." In 1900, C. M. Skinner, editor of the *Brooklyn Daily Eagle*, said, "Teeth will disappear seventy-five years from now, because the food of the future will be concentrated and made directly from chemicals so that there will be no strain on the digestion or gums." In 1963, the United States Secretary of Defense said, "The war in Vietnam is going well and will succeed."

Despite the propensity for error, it is vital for God's people to lean into the future with wisdom and flexibility, because just about anything could happen tomorrow. So in the following pages, we will gaze through seven portals into the days between now and the year 2025. I want to stress that I am in no way condoning or promoting any of the trends I will describe, since many of them are evil. But I am suggesting that if reformission takes hold, if God's people can see tomorrow and prepare for it today, some of the sinful things listed need not occur.

POPULATION

- The roughly eighty million people born between 1977 and 1997 will have more money to spend than even their parents did, making them the wealthiest generation in the history of the United States.[1]
- Americans will continue to live longer than even the average all-time high of 77.2 years set in 2001, causing the methods of everything from advertising to evangelism to change in order to connect with older people. By 2030, over half of the adults in the United States will be age fifty or older and qualify for membership in the AARP.[2]
- By 2025, there will be as many senior citizens over the age of sixty-five in America as there were African Americans in 2003.[3]
- The fifty million Americans born before 1945 — called the Builder generation because they created much of modern-day America, or what Tom Brokaw called the Greatest Generation — were very thrifty with their money following the Great Depression. They currently hold nearly two-thirds of all the nation's financial assets and will leave an estimated $41 trillion to their children and grandchildren, minus the 6 percent they will leave to charities, including churches and other ministries.[4]

- Members of future generations will be increasingly multiracial, a trend which will redefine traditionally accepted categories of race or will cause race to no longer be a defining factor of a person's identity.
- The number of immigrants will increase to 13 percent of the population. Hispanics will outnumber blacks by more than three to two, "minorities" will account for 40 percent of the population,[5] and the number of Asians will double to 7 percent of the population.[6]
- Because of longer lifespans, immigration, and steady birth rates, the U.S. population will increase by 25 percent to over 350 million people.[7]

FAMILY

- Homosexual couples will be permitted to legally marry, likely after their relationships are first permitted as a civil union or some other arrangement that would give same-sex couples some of the same legal benefits as married couples.
- It will become increasingly common for homosexual couples to have children through artificial insemination, surrogate mothering, adoption, and foster care.
- After homosexual-marriage legislation, or some other equivalent, has been passed, there will be a push for legalized polygamy in order to include bisexual people and their multiple partners as legitimate families.
- It will become increasingly common for traditional gender roles in the family to be reversed as many women become the sole or primary breadwinner and their husbands stay home to raise the children, leading to the further decline of strong men.
- Parents who want to have only one or two children will have "designer babies," selecting the traits they prefer to ensure that they get exactly what they want in a child.

- As more mothers work, either because they want to or have to, child-raising will be increasingly done by institutions such as daycares and year-round schools.

HEALTH AND MEDICINE

- While people die of starvation in other nations, American adults and children will continue eating themselves to death as obesity rates and related health problems rise.
- Alternative medicines and organic foods will become more mainstream as some Americans pursue alternatives to such things as medication and surgery.
- Increasing numbers of younger Americans will wear a permanent fashion accessory such as a tattoo or a body piercing other than a pierced ear.
- Elective and cosmetic surgeries and procedures will become increasingly common among both males and females in an effort to give the appearance of healthiness.
- Drug use will increasingly be viewed as a sickness rather than a crime, and as a result, it will be legalized, beginning with marijuana, and the money spent to fight the drug war will be reallocated to drug education, prevention, and treatment.
- Medical knowledge is currently doubling every eight years, and the speed of change in the medical field in the near future will be staggering.[8]
- Medical developments will outpace widespread public opinion on the ethics of such things as genetic engineering, cloning, DNA mapping, surrogate motherhood, infertility solutions, selection of a child's sex, use of fetal tissue, artificial organs, organ cloning, and life support.

CREATION

- There will be increased legislation to expand the legal rights of certain animals that are deemed close evolutionary relatives of humans and therefore deserving of nearly the same legal protections.

- Americans generate 4.3 pounds of trash per person each day. Our overall waste stream has tripled since 1970, and the Environmental Protection Agency states that by 2025, 70 percent of the nation's 2,200 landfills will be full. This development will result in legislation to mandate recycling and environmentally conscious business practices,[9] similar to what has been enacted in Seattle, which now recycles roughly half of its solid waste.[10]

- Ecoterrorist groups seeking to protect everything from animals to land will proliferate and become more brazen.

TECHNOLOGY

- Home entertainment will continue to flourish, making it possible for technohermits to rarely ever leave home.

- Radio will experience its most radical transformation since FM broadcasting began in 1946, as satellite radio will increase the number of free and premium channels, much like present-day cable-television channels.

- Internet gambling will pose for many gambling addicts an irresistible temptation because of its immediacy and anonymity and the difficulty of regulating it.

- Many businesses and some churches will be better known by their web address than by their physical address.

- All phones will be mobile, and use of the traditional home phone will cease.

- Bills and tithes will be paid digitally through online banking and digital credit, making cash and checks virtually obsolete.

- Churches will use their website as a new front door through which visitors will pass before ever attending a church event. People will even attend church virtually.

- Churches will create password-protected sections of their websites, or different sites altogether, for their members to chat online, share resources, exchange contact information, connect with church leaders, and so on, and churches will use e-mail chains in place of weekly printed bulletins.
- Technology will continue to reshape people in such a way that their attention spans will be shorter and they will have difficulty distinguishing truth and lies, and the deluge of information will become so great that separating the useful from the trivial will be laborious.
- The tsunami of information and services customized to please individual people will create a culture of self-absorbed, narcissistic people consumed with themselves and unconcerned about serving other people.

SEXUALITY

- Singleness will increase as more people postpone marriage, experience divorce, or forego marriage altogether.
- Cohabitation will become increasingly common as more people decide they don't want to get married but still want companionship and as more people want to test whether they are compatible for marriage.
- Immodest dress will become more brazen, even among young children (particularly girls), with undergarments and clothing styles that in previous generations would have been common only among prostitutes.
- Pornography and the sex industry will continue to drive and benefit from advances in technology and will push so far into mainstream culture that it will no longer be considered dirty or taboo.
- Deviant sexuality such as pedophilia and bestiality will not likely become more widely accepted but will become

more widely practiced through the increasing anonymity afforded by technology.

- Championed for reducing everything from disease to unwanted pregnancy to loneliness to sex crimes, technology will provide new sexual opportunities such as lifelike robots that function as sexual partners, and snugly fitting body suits containing electronic units that allow people separated by distance to have cybersex that feels like real sex.[11]

RELIGION

- There will be an increase in ancient pagan practices, much like those of the days of the Old Testament, made possible by the ability to share information, build communities, and create movements digitally.
- Demonic activity will rise and will increasingly be misdiagnosed as solely medical or psychological problems.
- Religious fanatics will increasingly resort to violence and terrorism to punish those who oppose them and to protect practices and ways of life they believe to be sacred.
- Mainline and liberal Protestant denominations will continue to slowly bleed to death.
- God will continue to seek worshipers, and Jesus will continue to save people from Satan, sin, and death in miraculous ways.

NOTES

INTRODUCTION

1. George Barna, "Unchurched Nation," *Moody Magazine* (July–August 2003), www.moodymagazine.com, accessed April 29, 2004.
2. The following discussion summarizes ideas from Lesslie Newbigin, *The Open Secret: An Introduction to the Theology of Mission* (Grand Rapids: Eerdmans, 1995), 153, and further expanded in the Gospel and Our Culture Network's book *The Church between Gospel and Culture*, ed. George Hunsberger (Grand Rapids: Eerdmans, 1996).

CHAPTER 1. EAT, DRINK, AND BE A MERRY MISSIONARY

1. 1 Corinthians 3:16–17; Ephesians 2:19–22.

CHAPTER 2. AND NOW, THE NEWS

1. Acts 10, 15; Romans 14–15; 1 Corinthians 10:14–33.

CHAPTER 3. SHOTGUN WEDDINGS TO JESUS

1. Acts 13:13–52; 17:16–34; 28:17–28.
2. George Hunter, *The Celtic Way of Evangelism: How Christianity Can Reach the West … Again* (Nashville: Abingdon, 2000).
3. James H. Gilmore and Joseph Pine II, *The Experience Economy* (Boston: Harvard Business School, 1999).
4. Romans 3:20–27; 5:19–21; 1 Corinthians 1:30; Titus 3:3–7.
5. Robert D. Putnam, *Bowling Alone: The Collapse and Revival of American Community* (New York: Simon and Schuster, 2000), 19.
6. Ibid., 66–67.
7. Ibid.
8. Ibid., 75–76.
9. Ibid.
10. Polly LaBarre, "How to Lead a Rich Life," *Fast Company,* March 2003, 74.

11. Putnam, *Bowling Alone,* 102–5.
12. Ibid., 101.
13. Ibid., 102.
14. Ibid., 105.
15. www.bowlingalone.com.
16. Putnam, *Bowling Alone,* 98, 100, 102–5.
17. www.bowlingalone.com.
18. Putnam, *Bowling Alone,* 112–13.
19. Ibid., 100.
20. Ibid., 150–51.
21. Ibid., 107.
22. Ibid.

CHAPTER 4. ELVIS IN EDEN

1. Rodney Clapp, *A Peculiar People: The Church as Culture in a Post-Christian Society* (Downers Grove, Ill.: InterVarsity, 1996), 74.
2. Renato Rosaldo, *Culture and Truth: The Remaking of Social Analysis* (Boston: Beacon, 1989), 25–26.
3. Lesslie Newbigin, *Foolishness to the Greeks: The Gospel and Western Culture* (Grand Rapids: Eerdmans, 1986), 3.
4. Ken Myers, *All God's Children and Blue Suede Shoes: Christians and Popular Culture* (Wheaton, Ill.: Crossway, 1989), 59–61, 90, 120.
5. Alvin Toeffler, *The Third Wave* (New York: Bantam, 1991).
6. James H. Gilmore and Joseph Pine II, *The Experience Economy* (Boston: Harvard Business School, 1999), 7–8.
7. Ibid.
8. Ibid., 8.
9. Robert D. Putnam, *Bowling Alone: The Collapse and Revival of American Community* (New York: Simon and Schuster, 2000), 169.
10. "Americans Embrace Technologies That Bring Control to Their Lives," April 1, 2003. Retrieved November 18, 2003 from http://www.barna.org /cgibin/PagePressRelease.asp?PressReleaseID=136&Reference=E&Key=technology.
11. Thomas Sowell, *A Conflict of Visions: Ideological Origins of Political Struggles* (New York: Basic, 2002).

CHAPTER 5. GOING TO SEMINARY AT THE GROCERY STORE

1. 1 John 2:15.
2. 1 John 2:17.
3. 1 John 3:1.
4. 1 John 3:13.
5. 1 John 4:1, 5.
6. James 1:27.
7. James 3:6.

8. James 4:4.
9. 1 Peter 2:11.
10. 2 Peter 1:4.
11. 1 Corinthians 1:20–21.
12. Romans 1:18–32.
13. 1 Corinthians 1:27–28.
14. Colossians 2:8; 2:20–3:3.
15. Ephesians 2:2, 12.
16. Galatians 3:22; 4:3.
17. 1 Corinthians 11:32.
18. John 1:1–18.
19. 1 John 4:9.
20. 1 John 4:4; 5:4–5.
21. Romans 12:2.
22. 2 Corinthians 10:3–4.
23. 1 John 4:17.
24. Bob Welanetz, "The Impact of Generation Y on Mall Ownership and Operations," *American Demographics* (December 2002–January 2003), insert between pages 52–53.

CHAPTER 6. THE SIN OF LIGHT BEER

1. Kenneth Gentry Jr., *God Gave Wine* (Lincoln, Calif.: Oakdown, 2001).
2. Ben Merkle, "Beer," *Credenda Agenda* 11 (April 6, 2000), 2.
3. Ibid.
4. Isaiah 1:22.
5. Psalm 75:8.
6. Numbers 6:3.
7. Gentry, *God Gave Wine,* 3–6.
8. John 2:1–11; Matthew 11:19.
9. Romans 14:21; 1 Corinthians 10:31–32.
10. Hosea 2:8.
11. Matthew 11:19.
12. 1 Timothy 4:1–5.
13. 1 Corinthians 10:31.
14. 1 Samuel 1:14, 24; 25:18, 37; Joel 1:9, 10.
15. Psalm 104:14–15; Ecclesiastes 9:7; 10:19.
16. Joel 2:24; Isaiah 25:6; 27:2–6; Jeremiah 31:12; Hosea 2:22; Joel 3:18; Amos 9:13–14.
17. Isaiah 16:10; Joel 1:5, 12.
18. Our church in Seattle partakes of communion every week and provides both juice and wine to permit people to obey their conscience on the matter.
19. Jim West, *Drinking with Calvin and Luther* (Lincoln, Calif.: Oakdown, 2003), 29.

CHAPTER 7. POSTMODERN PANDEMONIUM

1. Richard Cote, *Re-visioning Mission: The Catholic Church and Culture in Postmodern America* (Mahwah, N.J.: Paulist, 1996), 91.
2. Genesis 1:26–30; 9:1–2; 9:6–11; Psalm 8.
3. Huston Smith, *Beyond the Postmodern Mind* (Wheaton, Ill.: Theosophical, 1982).
4. Richard Rorty, interview by Michael Horton, "Truth, Evil, Redemption: A Neo-Pragmatist Perspective," *Modern Reformation,* July–August 2003, www.modernreformation.org, accessed April 29, 2004.
5. Polly LaBarre, "How to Lead a Rich Life," *Fast Company,* March 2003, 74.
6. John de Graaf, David Wann, and Thomas H. Naylor, *Affluenza: The All-Consuming Epidemic* (San Francisco: Berrett-Koehler, 2001), 4.
7. Ibid.
8. Ibid., 13.
9. Ibid., 41.
10. Ibid., 14.
11. Ibid., 15.
12. Ibid., 13.
13. Stanley J. Grenz, *A Primer on Postmodernism* (Grand Rapids: Eerdmans, 1996), 123–24.

CONCLUSION

1. Edward Cornish, "The Futurist Outlook 2001," *World Futures Society* (2000), 4.
2. Ibid., 7.
3. Alison Stein Wellner, "The Next Twenty-five Years," *American Demographics* (April 2003), 25.
4. Michael J. Weiss, "Great Expectations," *American Demographics* (May 2003), 27–35.
5. Jeffrey Passel, interviewed by Peter Fancese, "Consumers Today," *American Demographics* (April 2003), 33. Passel worked with the Census Bureau for fifteen years and is now a principal research associate at the Urban Institute in Washington, D.C.
6. Wellner, "The Next Twenty-five Years," 26.
7. Ibid., 28.
8. Marvin J. Cetron and Owen Davies, "Fifty Trends Now Changing the World," *World Futures Society* (2001), 16.
9. Ibid., 11–12.
10. Marvin J. Cetron and Owen Davies, "Trends Shaping the Future," *The Futurist* (January-February 2003), 40.
11. Edward Cornish, "The Cyber Future: Ninety-Three Ways Our Lives Will Change by 2005," *World Futures Society* (1999), 12.

Share Your Thoughts

With the Author: Your comments will be forwarded to the author when you send them to *zauthor@zondervan.com*.

With Zondervan: Submit your review of this book by writing to *zreview@zondervan.com*.

Free Online Resources at
www.zondervan.com

Zondervan AuthorTracker: Be notified whenever your favorite authors publish new books, go on tour, or post an update about what's happening in their lives at www.zondervan.com/authortracker.

Daily Bible Verses and Devotions: Enrich your life with daily Bible verses or devotions that help you start every morning focused on God. Visit www.zondervan.com/newsletters.

Free Email Publications: Sign up for newsletters on Christian living, academic resources, church ministry, fiction, children's resources, and more. Visit www.zondervan.com/newsletters.

Zondervan Bible Search: Find and compare Bible passages in a variety of translations at www.zondervanbiblesearch.com.

Other Benefits: Register to receive online benefits like coupons and special offers, or to participate in research.

ZONDERVAN

ZONDERVAN.com/
AUTHORTRACKER
follow your favorite authors